DONALD W. WINNICOTT

DONALD W. WINNICOTT
A New Approach

Laura Dethiville

Translated by Susan Ganley Lévy

KARNAC

First published in 2008 in French by Editions Campagne Première as *Donald W. Winnicott: Une nouvelle approche*

First published in English in 2014 by
Karnac Books Ltd
118 Finchley Road
London NW3 5HT

British Library Cataloguing in Publication Data

A C.I.P. for this book is available from the British Library

ISBN-13: 978-1-78220-165-6

Typeset by V Publishing Solutions Pvt Ltd., Chennai, India

www.karnacbooks.com

For Stéphane

CONTENTS

ACKNOWLEDGEMENTS

With thanks to all who have accompanied the writing of this book:

to Yvette Lemaire and Marie Lacôte, who were able to decipher
my handwriting and my scraps of paper;

to Cécile Lathière-Jaloux, who accompanied me
during its development;

to Mike Lévy, whose talent and creativity helped me
to formulate highly abstract notions;

and finally, to François Lévy, my partner in this adventure.
Thank you for your unfailing support, patience and effectiveness.

ABOUT THE AUTHOR

Laura Dethiville, psychoanalyst, full member and vice-president of the Société de Psychanalyse Freudienne, has been running a seminar on Winnicott for over fifteen years. She has written two books, *D.W.W Une nouvelle approche*, and *La Clinique de Winnicott*, both published with Editions Campagne-Première, numerous papers in several reviews, and has participated in many collected works. *D.W.W Une nouvelle approche* has been translated in Portuguese, Chinese, Italian, and English.

INTRODUCTION

As part of the group who founded the Société de psychanalyse freudienne in 1994, I volunteered to lead a seminar on the work of Donald W. Winnicott. However, in spite of my enthusiasm, I quickly put certain of his texts aside after reading the French translation of one of his books. The following summer I visited Maresfield Gardens, where I bought *Through Paediatrics to Psycho-Analysis* and *The Maturational Processes and the Facilitating Environment*. I later acquired all the others, in particular *Psycho-Analytic Explorations*, and I discovered a Winnicott I had not suspected.

When all's said and done, it is quite a common experience, shared by many. As always, a translation is already an interpretation and certain shades of meaning don't pass from one language to another. Something is always lost in translation.

I was able to brush up on my knowledge of Winnicott and complete it by referring to the work of those he does not always cite, but whose findings he calls on: Freud, of course, but also Sandor Ferenczi, Melanie Klein, Wilfred R. Bion, Ronald Fairbairn, and Phyllis Greenacre.

I gradually discovered an indefatigable researcher, an exacting mind, constantly ready to question his findings when new elements appeared during clinical studies. This was the work pattern of his whole life, not adding new elements to an established theory, but going beyond current theories and thus adhering closely to his own clinical experience. On reading his texts, we realise how much he modified his way of working over the years. He acknowledges it himself:

> It appals me to think how much deep change I have prevented or delayed in patients *in a certain classification category* by my personal need to interpret. If only we can wait, the patient arrives at understanding creatively and with immense joy, and I now enjoy this joy more than I used to enjoy the sense of having been clever. I think I interpret mainly to let the person know the limits of my understanding. The principle is that it is the patient and only the patient who has the answers. (Winnicott, 1971a)

At the insistence of his wife, he had started on his autobiography just before his death. Even though he had only completed a few pages, he had already chosen the title: *Not Less than Everything*. An eloquent title, which makes us feel infinitely humble.

Consequently, when I attempted to write up the results developed during my seminars at the Société de psychanalyse freudienne and numerous later conferences, the task was not easy. To try to fix—or define—the salient points of such a changing, animated thought process ran the risk of draining it of everything it encompassed, the living proof of its creativity.

It is impossible to "define" Winnicott's concepts. We can only relate them. They have a life of their own, and often all we can do is follow them, making sure that we are not lost along the way.

This book is taking up the challenge; to try and "relate" Winnicott, at the same time updating his intuitions in the light of present-day discoveries.

CHAPTER ONE

Winnicott today

In France there is a deep misunderstanding of Donald W. Winnicott. He is well known, in fact extremely well known, but at the same time not completely understood. His work was met with considerable interest in the 1970s, due to the success of the concept of the transitional object. But this success fell flat, not without some damage. Flat is the word, since his ideas were completely squashed. For the most part, his work was either politely ignored, or considered banal, uninteresting, and meaningless. Winnicott today is referred to even by those not hostile to his ideas as "the nice man who has worked on the mother–baby relationship, and with children, and who says that he does not need to call on the death instinct theory in his work."

And so it was for many years, and then things changed. At the moment, Winnicott is back in fashion. His ideas are being taken up by psychoanalysts from different schools of thought, and he seems to be approved of unanimously by these different trends, which in turn poses numerous questions. Personally, I feel that most of the time his work is the object of a misunderstanding. He is forever being quoted, several of his concepts are taken up as slogans, and at the same time, it is not sure that we fully estimate the upheaval that he has brought to

1

both the theory and the practical sides of therapy. Although reference is abundantly made to his work, it remains largely unknown. We have to admit that the essential parts of his work have only recently been translated into French, work which was published after his death, and which marks the final progress of his thought.

Winnicott died at the age of seventy-four from a heart condition, shortly after supervising the publication of *Playing and Reality* (1971a). He left behind an impressive amount of unpublished material, which has been gradually published by the Winnicott Trust and the Winnicott Publications Committee.

Clinical learning

Winnicott was a demanding analyst, difficult, inventive, and—which is less usual—capable of revising his ideas as a consequence of interaction with a patient, accepting it, allowing himself to be challenged in his established theoretic certainties. The dedication of *Playing and Reality*: "To my patients who have paid to teach me", reveals his openness, his extraordinary faculty of acceptance. In "A personal view of the Kleinian contribution" (1962a), he recounts how he realised very early on in his consultations with children that, as opposed to the traditional theory that the origin of neurotic fixations stemmed from the Oedipus complex, "there was something somewhere which was not right". He encountered children [*infans*] who showed very precocious symptoms in their life. And he confided: "I'm going to show that infants are ill very early and if the theory doesn't fit it, it's just got to adjust itself. So that was that" (Winnicott, 1967c, p. 575).

We have equally at our disposition a short piece, written in 1967: "D.W.W. on D.W.W". This text is the transcription of an informal talk given at the Club 52, a small group of analysts who used to meet far from the "Controversies" of the British Society of Psychoanalysts. We can feel Winnicott is relaxed, at ease, almost intimate, discussing with his close colleagues, having reached a time in his life when he feels calm and sure of his opinions. With great humility and simplicity he describes his experimentations and the long period of clinical proof which he needed to integrate certain facts. For example, he says, "It took me three or four years to come to the simple fact that there are two sorts of deprivation" (ibid., p. 575).

During the course of this talk, he pronounces a touching phrase concerning his formation and its course. He asks, "So when did I start to wake up a little?" (ibid., p. 575)—a phrase which alludes to the way in which he had to unlearn everything he "knew", to be able to be himself.

He worked until his dying day to complete the theory that had emerged throughout the years from his clinical experience. It shows continually evolving, original and creative thought (just as he had the same idea of a constantly evolving subject). This is perhaps why the sense of his concepts constantly evolved between the beginning and end of his work. For this reason we should remain extremely vigilant to avoid confusion, and it is not certain that he himself was not occasionally confused.

A scattered corpus

Winnicott's work is therefore not easy to approach. Talking about his work he observes: "it has meant that what I've said has been isolated and people have had to do a lot of work to get at it" (ibid., p. 575). It is a wonderful comparison that warns us that we may have to work hard at it. First and foremost his work is bitty, composed of small articles often aimed at very different audiences. He loved to address very different types of audience, and he adapted his style accordingly, refusing to use meta-psychological terms as often as possible.

The books that have been published try to put together these articles and lectures in a logical fashion. His sole attempt to standardise an atomised corpus appeared in *Human Nature* (1988), a large part of which he wrote in 1954, completing a second synopsis around 1957, and which he was continually reworking until his death.

Therefore we have an unfinished version at our disposal, a version complete with his handwritten notes. We really do not know exactly what he would have wished to keep.

The difficulties of translation

The paradox of this man, gifted with great inventiveness, inclined to create his own concepts, his own metaphors, skilful at invention and play on words in English, was that he could also be very "conventional"—even compliant—in his use of terminology. In particular he conforms to the psychoanalytic vocabulary in use at the time, but imparts a very subtle difference. As he explains himself, "The invention of a new word would have been less easily justified than the treatment of an already existing word with a splash of paint" (Winnicott, 1935, p. 129). But as I mentioned above, this "splash of paint", however imperceptible, can lead to a real "misunderstanding", if we read too hurriedly.

Last but not least, the translation of this very personal language poses great difficulty. We often have to resolve not to translate, or need to turn a phrase into something which may sound clumsy, but which is closer to the English sense. With the problem of translating from one language to another and the confusion created by Winnicott's lack of precision, it is often difficult to make sense.

For example, take the concepts of "ego", "self", and false self. All his life Winnicott used "self", "ego", "psychic reality" or "psyche" indifferently and with little precision (this adds to the difficulties when translating his work into French), and it is only in the last ten years of his life that he really refined his position.

First we must remember that the English have chosen to translate the German *ich* as *ego*, a subjective pronoun in a dead language which does not render the subjectivity represented by the *ich* in German and the *je* in French.

In his texts Winnicott uses either *ego* or *me* in a very defined way. *Me* is a term he uses to indicate the idea of an internal subjective experience, whereas *ego* is the subject talking, the conscious "me"—and this, again, causes complications in a French text where *"moi"* is used in both cases.

Moreover, in a letter to his translator concerning the difficulties she has in translating the word "self", he writes: "the self which is not the ego", which we generally find translated as: *"le self qui n'est pas le moi"*. Further in the same text, he uses *me* in a completely different sense, and he has no option but to translate it once more as *"moi"*. In the face of such difficulty, certain translators chose to cite the English term in brackets. Thus in the excellent translation of *Human Nature*, when Winnicott mentions the differentiation between the *"moi"* and *"non-moi"*, the translator goes to the trouble of indicating that in the text, Winnicott uses *me* and *not-me*, and not *ego*.

These notions of self, false self, and ego, so essential to Winnicott, are of an extremely important subtlety. When we study his work closely, and in spite of contradictions, we find that the "me", the "ego" is an organising principle of the "self", but only a part, the "self" being composed of interpenetrating parts. We will come back to this later.

In fact, we find that he leads us into quite another meta-psychology, different from the Freudian meta-psychology, a meta-psychology which shakes the classical theory. It is perhaps for this reason that it is preferable to keep to a certain approximation. Otherwise Winnicott's observations could appear "rather shocking".

On another level, the simplicity with which Winnicott recounts certain things makes them seem so evident that we get the impression we have always known them. This familiarity is in fact a trap.

This simple, almost concrete language can create the illusion of immediate comprehension, but it is only an illusion. In fact it is terribly complex, and we have to admit that sometimes it is difficult to understand. One of his famous phrases has been endlessly quoted. He pronounced it after a Working Party at the British Society in 1942, (and only wrote it down a decade later) when he had been particularly annoyed by what he had heard: "There is no such thing as a baby" (Winnicott, 1952a, p. 99) which can be roughly translated as "A thing that we call a baby doesn't exist", which is to say that we cannot speak about a baby without also considering the environment he is part of, who is carrying him, looking at him, the voice surrounding him, the transitional space he creates, etc. This will be the major originality of his findings and his important stroke of genius. He gradually comes to understand the mechanisms at work in what we call the constitution of human psyche, beginning with an infant-environment entity from which the human being can slowly develop his identity.

He thus describes the way to access subjectivity in our relationship to the other (other and the Other).

The "good enough" mother and the importance of environment

We should break off here to consider the misunderstanding of the term "a good enough mother". I insist on this because it seems that the expression has had a prejudicial effect on the way the French approach Winnicott. It has become a kind of slogan in psychoanalytical language. And this idea of a mother who is "good enough"—Winnicott's often talked about "good enough mother"—has altered our understanding of what Winnicott has brought to a rather silly psychologism, concerning the illusion of a possible appropriateness of the mother to the needs of the child, appropriateness which remains the ideal mother–child relationship. In this way Winnicott has been accused of making mothers feel guilty.

When Winnicott uses the expression "good enough mother" there is no problem in English. "Good enough" is that which is "just good", "passable",[1] "just enough", no more. For him the *good enough* mother is just an ordinary mother, adequate, nothing else. On the 31st July 1969 he wrote to Helm Stierlin: "You use the words *good experience*. It is important to me that in my writings I always say *good-enough* rather than *good*. I think that the words *good-enough* help to steer the reader away from sentimentality and idealisation" (Winnicott, 1987a, p. 195).

Winnicott always resists any sentimentality, since sentimentality seems to him to go hand in hand with a certain misunderstanding of hate—which risks bringing dire consequences. At the end of his life he preferred to use the term mother-environment, and he spoke generally of an environment that includes the "others" of the mother, particularly the father, but also the family, social reality, etc. The environment, the mother-environment, at that point, is for him a function even if it is also a subject. The child [*infans*] is not conscious of this environment. It is taken for granted. It is unknown and will probably never be known. It can only be known negatively, as something lacking.

In fact the environment only becomes apparent when it is missing. The essential principle is that by a good enough adaptation to his needs, the individual can "be" and does not have to know anything about the environment. We do not remember about being held. We keep trace in our memory of the experience of having been dropped.

What is so particular about Winnicott is that he thought about the way in which "an environment we can rely upon allows us to establish a place to retire to, to simply be" (Winnicott, 1960a, p. 37).

And he was often criticised for having reintroduced into psychoanalysis the idea of "being", and "going on being", in the manner of phenomenological philosophers. In an environment that holds correctly, the baby is able to accomplish a personal development according to his "inherited potential". He experiments a "continuity of being" which eventually transforms into a feeling of existing, a sentiment of unified self, and he comes to what Winnicott calls unit-status, that is, an individual who comes to successful indwelling. Therefore the mother does not have to be "good" but simply "fair". He states that a mother who is too good has a devastating effect on the child: "In this way the mother, being a seemingly good mother, does something worse than castrate the infant. The latter is left with two alternatives: either being a permanent state of regression and of being merged with the mother, or else staging a total rejection of the mother, even of the seemingly good mother" (Winnicott, 1960a, p. 51).

On the other hand, Winnicott always insists that the baby has his own activity. He immediately acknowledges the baby's ability to catalogue, sort out, etc. and thus to think, a capacity to think which is present from the beginning. In this sense, he is a precursor, closely followed today, for example, by Daniel Stern and his work, and his hypotheses are currently totally confirmed.

The majority of Winnicott's views should not be taken up in the psychological perspective of "good" or "bad" mothering, but from the point of view of a tiny human being who comes into the world endowed with the power to organise his world, a world which he is going to have to face to make it his own (according to Roustang, 1994. This is Winnicott's "found–created" which we will come to later.) And this world (including himself) is presented to him by his environment, an environment he is part of. (It is from the other that the meaning will come. From the start, everything is mediatised.)

This relationship to the other takes place in the transitional space, a fantastic discovery by Winnicott, a space neither inside nor outside and where all we ask is to exist, a space in-between, which becomes the place to relate to the world, the place in fact of a creative perception (apperception) of the world. For there is no other relationship to the other or to the world than in this found–created space.

Ruthless/ruthlessness

Ruthless is an old English word which does not mean "cruel", but rather "disregarding the other, having no compassion". Winnicott uses this term when he speaks of the period before what he calls "the stage of concern", which corresponds more or less to the "depressive position" of Melanie Klein. At that precise moment, he says, the infant is *ruthless*. He also talks about his *ruthless love*. He says that an infant can seem without regard for the other, but simply because at that moment the other has not materialised as such! Moreover Winnicott's vocabulary here is very precise. He does sometimes use the words "cruel" and "cruelty", but it is always in connection with adults, either in environment or observation. Therefore the newborn is not cruel, he is without regard.

This is a very important point, since we often see confusion or an amalgam with Melanie Klein's the "cruel infant". Winnicott's views dissociate clearly and decisively from the Kleinian position. The infant will go from the "pre-ruth" stage to the "ruth" stage. It is of course an intra-psychic process, but it is a process which supposes that there is an adequate environment (another human being) for it to be accomplished. At the same time, the infant can constitute the other as such by the way he progressively detaches himself. By creating the other, the infant can overcome the lack of differentiation in which he was evolving to reach what Winnicott calls the stage of concern. As Winnicott so nicely puts it, if the infant could one day look back to that period, he might say: "I was ruthless then."

Meeting needs

We must also include a term which poses a great problem for the French: the word "need". Once again, the problem arises from the passage from one language to another, but it also concerns the meta-psychological. In fact we should say "necessities". It is not about answering needs—we know that it is not enough to obtain the psychic satisfaction necessary for the self-fulfilment of a person—but to seek what is necessary, and it is therefore indispensable to meet the needs. Of course in English *to want* first means "to be without" and then "to desire". *He is in want* means "he knows what he is missing". That which is lacking is what we need. So we understand that satisfaction in a hallucinatory mode comes from obtaining ourselves what is missing. And here again we find the same problems with translation, both from German to English in the *Standard Edition*, and from English to French.

Freud mentions briefly the great "needs", the *Bedürfnisse*—hunger, thirst, sexuality—which from a biological point of view must be satisfied absolutely. When it comes to "needs", Winnicott does not consider the instinct of id impulse. "A need is either met or not met, and the effect is not the same as that of satisfaction or frustration of id impulse." And an inadequacy in the environment at that moment generates neither anger nor even frustration, but rather "an unthinkable anxiety", that is, an anxiety which cannot be thought of and will always be unthinkable.

Anxiety and primitive agony

Anxiety, as we see it, cannot be a condition at the beginning of life. To exist, anxiety requires a minimum of egotic. So if there is anxiety at that moment, it must be that of the mother. And this anxiety (the mother's) will pervade her whole relationship with the infant, and will be felt by him through a multitude of discreet signals.

This is how Winnicott at the beginning of his work began to use the term "anxiety", and this term continues to designate "neurotic anxiety". However he finds this term insufficient to describe disorganising, annihilating distress at the beginning of life. He prefers the term "agony", even "primitive agony", "a term which encompasses the word death" (Winnicott, 1956, p. 300). It is an experience of explosion, disintegration, annihilation. Unthinkable or archaic anxiety marks the period at the very beginning, before thought. Something which is unthinkable and can undoubtedly never be thought of but simply re-lived in analysis.

So we have an experience of annihilation which can neither be thought of nor integrated and against which will come up various different defences (primitive, archaic defences), defences which we will study: the exacerbation of mental function, the construction of false self, the organisation of chaos, compulsive fantasying. For Winnicott, anxiety is a positive signal, a signal of a defence, which is effective against the danger of agony. For him, a baby is constantly on the verge of an unthinkable anxiety, which we cannot begin to imagine.

As Wilfred R. Bion states in his *Learning from Experience* (1962), what a baby needs at this stage of his life is the maternal capacity to receive, contain, and transform, so that the baby can integrate it, the impulsive movements whose violence can be damaging for him.

We come across the same anxieties in psychotic patients (and this is how we can have an idea of what the baby experiences), or during psychotic attacks, and often also in dreams. It is also the experience of patients who have survived a serious, life-threatening crisis.

If there is a sudden change that is not accompanied by maternal empathy enabling the infant to find an adequate rhythm, or by the mother's voice warning of something about to happen—a voice enveloping the infant during this moment—this can bring about the threat of annihilation, splitting. This is the "ego-coverage", not the mother's ego-coverage but ego-coverage by the mother. So on many occasions, the passage from one language to another has given the French reader the "little splash of paint" which was needed, without there being an error in the translation.

The immobilisation of the adolescent

And so it is for the term doldrums, which Winnicott uses in his texts on adolescence.

Winnicott, born in Plymouth, was a good sailor. Doldrums is a maritime term which describes the time and place when a boat is completely becalmed, because there is no wind. We do not know which way the wind will blow, or even if it will blow at all. However there is movement in these calm waters. Winnicott implies that it is a moment of immobility, of re-evaluation, just as he will later say in *Therapeutic Consultations in Child Psychiatry* (1971g) that in analysis, such moments appear as a pause, a hesitation, which generally indicate the beginning of a passage from one state to another (This idea was first taken up by him during his observation of the spatula game. See Winnicott, 1941).

It is also the reason why we should emphasise the aspect of "time to go forward" which these periods represent so frequently in adolescence. This precision is important: we do not cure a crisis in adolescence. We accompany it. And it means that the therapist needs to know how to wait. But waiting does not mean being inactive. These different topics will come up later.

So it transpires from these remarks that for Winnicott, the human subject is formed from a primary infant-environment unit. Each human being possesses a capacity to move and transform, which is present all his life. We may qualify Winnicott a "naïve optimist", or of "naïve optimism", but he was truly convinced that, as long we could provide someone with an adequate environment, he would always strive to return to the moment when "his future stopped or the situation was frozen" (Winnicott, 1954a, p. 278).

In fact, Winnicott continually insisted on what he considered to be an essential faculty of the human being, which is his ability to take a spontaneous path to a healing if he is given the possibility to do so.

Of course this position implies a very original relation to the therapy and the transfer. For Winnicott, the cure was not only a "recollection", a rereading, or an interpretation of what happened, because, as we will see later, the spoken word can act as a defence. Language is of course our tool. But it can prove inadequate.

The psychoanalytic cure, as seen by Winnicott, is more a way of experimenting—for the first time perhaps—what had not until then been experienced. "The cure is a way to experiment the self, not to get to know it, not to cure" (Winnicott, 1989). The patient has to experience what perhaps he was not able to experience and this in the *hic et nunc* of the transfer relationship. It has not to do with "repair", but something that might happen that could not have taken place, or that something is registered which could not have registered, because the subject had not (or not yet) reached that stage. It would mean that a psychic event had occurred which could start the frozen processes off again (unfreezing). Is it not this the analytical act, a fertile, creative moment in the here and now?

Note

1. Passable: "capable of getting the child to where he should go, just enough to enable something to happen which must happen" according to Roger D'Orazio.

CHAPTER TWO

The man and his life

U ntil quite recently, the publications devoted to Winnicott seem to agree that he had a privileged childhood, in a comfortable environment, which favoured the fulfilment of his potential creativity. Only a few commentators seem to have picked up on an important theme which is a common thread running through his work.

The secret scar

This theme is that of "The manic defence", the title of a presentation given in 1935 in his application for membership of the British Psychoanalytical Society, a presentation that was not published until 1957. In this text he describes the psychic organisation of subjects who, from childhood, have played the role of therapist to their depressed mothers. These "parent" children had to ignore their own needs in order to be able to devote themselves to the difficult task of reviving their depressive mother. It is as if each of these children said to themselves "any minute the mother's face will become fixed or her mood will dominate, and my own personal needs must then be withdrawn otherwise my central self may suffer insult." And for example in "Reparation in respect of mother's organised defence against depression", he notes that the main task of these children is "to deal with mother's mood" (Winnicott, 1948, p. 93).

However—and we will see this in the chapter devoted to the depressive state—this continual task leaves hardly any place for the development of their own depressive state.

It would appear that Winnicott had knowledge of this, the unconscious knowledge which drove him all his life, a relentless, almost pathological searching, as far as his work was concerned. What was this gay dog, this cheerful Winnicott hiding? What was he attempting to cure during his two long analyses (very long for that time), ten years with James Strachey, five years with Joan Rivière? It is thanks to Adam Phillips's biography published in 1988 that we learn that behind the apparent idyll of a happy and balanced childhood, little Donald seems to have had the difficult experience of having to look after a depressive mother.

The big house in Plymouth, an idealised vision

Donald Woods Winnicott was born in 1898 into a rich Plymouth family. The first—and only—boy following two girls, he was brought up in a big house full of life and activity, set in a park, which was a wonderful place of exploration and adventure for the children. His first name, Donald, has its origin in an old Celtic word meaning "powerful" (Woods is the maiden name of his mother).

On the other side of the road lived his cousins, and the two families formed a dynamic group enjoying both great liberty and a sure and discreet protection. As one of his sisters says, "At home we never heard the question: 'What can I do?' There was always something to do, space to do it and someone to do it with us, if necessary."

This is why Winnicott is so often described as a much-loved child, growing up in a stable and secure environment.

Clare Winnicott, his second wife, recounts:

> The D. W. Winnicott household was a large and lively one with plenty of activity. But there was space for everyone in the large garden and house and there was no shortage of money. There is no doubt that the Winnicott parents were the centre of their children's lives, and that the vitality and stability of the entire household

emanated from them. Their mother was vivacious and outgoing and was able to show and express her feelings easily. (1965, p. 5)

This is an idyllic account, considering it comes from Clare. As she admitted herself, "this appears too good to be true, but it was so". We have to note however that Clare Winnicott "reconstructed" this atmosphere from the recollections and confidences of both her husband and her two sisters-in-law to whom she was very close—sisters-in-law who incidentally never married. And it is important to remember that Clare Winnicott never met Elizabeth, Donald's mother, who died in 1925.

A very feminine universe

However there is no doubt that the youngest child was spoilt and adored by a congregation of women—his mother, his sisters, the aunts who lived there and the domestic staff, including his "Nanni", to whom he remained very attached.

Young Donald was therefore brought up by his "multiple mothers", his expression. Recalling his "Nanni", Clare Winnicott recounts: "and one of the first things I remember doing with him years later in London was to seek her out and ensure that she was all right and living comfortably" (1965, p. 6).

His father, Frederick Winnicott, who was for a long time the mayor of Plymouth, was always very occupied with both his own business matters and those of the town. He was therefore often absent, so Donald lived almost exclusively in the company of women. In particular he loved to be in the kitchen, an eminently feminine area at the time, incurring the displeasure of his mother, who felt he spent too much time there (Clare Winnicott recalled later that during their travels, Winnicott always began by rushing into the kitchen of the hotels they stayed in, and that it was always there that she could find him).

Winnicott had undeniably a strong female identification and there is no doubt that this almost exclusive feminine configuration of his family was the origin. Winnicott had a very high-pitched voice, which he thoroughly detested. He used to give talks on the BBC, and stemming from the fact that he dealt essentially with the mother–baby relationship, his listeners often imagined that it was a women talking, and addressed their letters to "Mrs Winnicott". In *Clinical Notes on Disorders of Childhood*, Winnicott makes this clinical remark: "Sometimes a boy at puberty cannot use the new power of manly speech, but either must speak falsetto, or else unconsciously imitate the voice of a girl or woman he has known" (Winnicott, 1931, p. 119). He himself recounts, as if he wanted to reveal something hidden: "that in the early years [my father] left me too much to all my mothers. Things never quite righted themselves" (Clare Winnicott, 1965, p. 8). It is obvious that this familiarity with the feminine world, this profound capacity to identify with the "maternal" was the ferment of his research. Like the "devoted mother", he spent some fifty years of his life following his line of thought with passion and obstinacy, continually unravelling his ideas, and delving into the multiple facets of the first moment in the life of an individual. And contrary to what we sometimes think, it is more in his work with adults in the phase of profound regression that his experience as a paediatrician proved invaluable. He read very little of the work of his colleagues, but he had a way all his own of profiting from the findings of his peers. "What happens is that I gather this and that, here and there, settle down to clinical experience, form my own theories and then, last of all, interest myself in looking to see where I stole what" (Rodman, 2003). The accounts of those who knew him—friends, colleagues, fellow pupils—unanimously describe a lively, bright person, a little eccentric, sparkling with intelligence and gifted with a considerable artistic talent. He was funny and warm-hearted.

A depressive mother and the task of caring for her?

At the approach of old age, Winnicott wrote a poem ("The Tree") about his mother, which he sent to his brother-in-law, James Britton, accompanied by the following: "Do you mind seeing this hurt coming out of me? I think it had some thorns sticking out somehow. It's not happened to me before and I hope it doesn't again" (Kahr, 1996). These verses, apart from being deeply moving, give us another perspective of little Donald's childhood. The poem ("Mother below is weeping/Weeping"; Rodman, 2003, p. 289) seems to show that Elizabeth Winnicott suffered from depression and that as a child he had to use much of his energy to try and revive her psychically, something he will describe so well later on.

Years afterwards, Margaret Little will confirm that little Donald experienced his mother's frequent depressive episodes, and Winnicott himself hints that his father, who was too busy with his business to look after her, subconsciously gave him the responsibility of looking after his mother.

This interpretation throws new light on how he must have felt when sent off to boarding school at the age of thirteen: a terrible wrench, certainly, but also relief as well as guilt at not having accomplished his mission: "caring for his mother". Incidentally, do we not become a psychoanalyst because we failed in our first therapy, that of our mother? (An expression of Amaro de Villanova). We can quote Winnicott once more in *Hate in the Counter-Transference* (1947, p. 196): "Analysis is my chosen job, the way I feel I will best deal with my own guilt, the way I can express myself in a constructive way." A letter written by Winnicott at the age of 13, for Mother's Day, shows us the consideration he was capable of:

> My dearest mother,
>
> On September 2nd all true Scouts think of their mothers, since that was the birthday of Baden Powell's mother when she was alive.
>
> And so when you get this letter I shall be thinking of you in particular, and I hope you will get it in the morning.
>
> But to please me very much I must trouble you to do me a little favour. Before turning over the page I want you to go up into my bedroom and in the right-hand cupboard find a small parcel … Now, have you opened it? Well I hope you will like it. You can change it at Pophams if you don't. Only if you do so, you must ask to see No.1 who knows about it.
>
> I have had a ripping holiday, and I cannot thank you enough for what you have done and for your donation to the Scouts.
>
> My home is a beautiful home and I only wish I could live up to it.
>
> [...]
>
> But, it being Mother's day, most love goes to you,
>
> From your loving boy,
> Donald. (Clare Winnicott, 1965, p. 9)

It is not surprising that a child capable of buying a gift for his mother, and then giving her the instructions for her to find it, could later develop the idea of found–created.

The boarding school years

In his recollections, Winnicott recounts that at the age of nine he looked at himself in the mirror and decided that he had had enough of being good. According to him, there then followed a complicated period of bad school marks. He also tells us that later he had what must have been an albeit relatively turbulent adolescence. Once more the famous anecdote recounted by Winnicott that Frederick Winnicott sent him to boarding school after hearing him swear (the word "drat") must be put down to myth.

It is more likely that his father had realised that it was time to take him away from the almost exclusively feminine world in which he had evolved up until then, and give him a typical English education at Boarding School. But for the young Winnicott, it was surely important to feel he had finally found a father, a third party between him and his mother. So he was sent off to Leys School in Cambridge.

In his memoirs, he commits a lapsus when he states that he left when he was thirteen when in fact he was fourteen (September 1910). He was doubtless revealing the great vulnerability he felt at the time. And yet, even at the end of his life, he confides to his second wife: "Thank God I was sent away at the age of thirteen."

His sisters took over in looking after their mother. Neither one nor the other managed to gain independence from the family. They never married, devoting themselves to painting, piano, and singing. Music was very important in Winnicott's education and the whole family was musical. He played the piano very well and sang as a tenor. He cultivated these gifts all his life. The research undertaken by Brett Kahr gives us the picture of a lively boy, rather popular, at ease with the other pupils and teachers, fond of sports and a fine musician.

At the age of sixteen, he suffered a broken clavicle, and from then on he was determined to be a doctor: "I could see that for the rest of my life I should have to depend on doctors if I damaged myself or became ill" (Clare Winnicott, 1965, p. 10).

His medical vocation

We can puzzle over this quasi-phobia of dependence which he felt his whole life. It is probably what protected him from any indoctrination and explains in part his difficulties with Melanie Klein. We also wonder what the danger was he was trying to escape from, he who could demonstrate so well how painful it is to the patient "to be dependent unless one is actually an infant" (Winnicott, 1963c, p. 240).

This choice of a medical career was also (and possibly above all) a way of choosing to distance himself from his father, a man who was extremely influential in the town (he was in fact knighted in 1924). Frederick Winnicott had hoped of course that his son would take his place in the successful family business. To become a doctor ensured that the young man could avoid this predetermined fate, so he continued his studies at Jesus College, Cambridge.

It was at about this time that Winnicott became an Anglican, he who had been brought up in a Methodist family, albeit non-conformist. He never mentioned the why nor wherefore of this decision.

War and the survivor's guilt

At the declaration of the First World War in 1914, the English colleges were transformed into military hospitals. Since he was a medical student, Donald Winnicott was exempted from military service, and saw his fellow students leave for the Front. Several of his close friends were killed at the outbreak of hostilities, which affected Donald for the rest of his life. Clare Winnicott recounts how "he always felt that he had a responsibility to live for those who died, as well as for himself" (Clare Winnicott, 1965, p. 11). He himself noted: "I have never been free from the feeling that my being alive is a facet of some another [sic] thing of which their deaths can be seen as another facet of some huge crystal, a body with integrity and shape intrinsic to it" (This phrase appears in a draft of the biography which Winnicott started working on at the insistence of his wife Clare, and which he wanted to call *Not Less than Everything*). Today we call this "the survivor's guilt".

However he quickly managed to get himself enlisted in the Navy— which is only natural for a native of Plymouth—and was appointed as a trainee surgeon on board a destroyer. He had little medical experience, but fortunately he was assisted by an experienced male nurse. He wrote to his mother with his usual humour: "I'm only here to reassure the sailors' mothers that their boys had a doctor on board" (Kahr, 1996, p. 30). At the end of the war, he finished his medical studies. His intention was to become a general practitioner and set up in the country. But having read one of Freud's books, he was drawn to psychoanalysis.

First marriage and the beginning of his analysis

After qualifying in 1920, he was granted, in 1923, two hospital posts: one at the Queen Elizabeth Hospital for Children, and the other at Paddington Green Children's Hospital where he worked for forty years. The same year he started his private practice, where he received hospital patients whom he considered needed longer consultations. According to his second wife, Winnicott said it was also to impress the porter, and he even went as far as to pay the taxi for his poorer patients. He was therefore already working with children and their families, but he still depended on the financial support of his father.

In the same year—in July 1923—he married Alice Buxton Taylor, who had a history of psychiatric illness. Masud Khan would say "she was a singer who had gone mad", and of Winnicott, "taking care of her took all his youth."

It seems that the couple experienced marital difficulties from the beginning and at the end of 1923, Winnicott started a personal analysis with James Strachey. He will simply say. "I was ill". It would be indecent to speculate on the kind of difficulties that Winnicott had, although James Strachey did reveal a great deal in his correspondence with his wife Alix, thus violating professional secrecy. Since the principal source of information on Winnicott's life comes from his second wife, Clare Winnicott, we know very little of this first marriage, which nevertheless lasted twenty-five years.

Although he had met Clare Britton during the Second World War, he only divorced in 1949, after the death of his father, the year in which he also had his first heart attack. According to Brett Kahr (1996), Winnicott exhausted himself trying to care for his first wife, and it was a long time before he abandoned hope. At the same time, these years corresponded to his formation and to intense upheavals, both in his analysis and his professional experience.

From paediatry to psychoanalysis

He writes: "At the beginning there was myself learning to do analysis as a paediatrician [...] having had great difficulty in seeing a baby as human at all. It was only through analysis that I became gradually able to see a baby as a human being" (Winnicott, 1967c, p. 574).

Winnicott was not a paediatrician who turned to psychoanalysis, as was often thought. *He was a consultant in a hospital for children, whose work was transformed by his personal experience of psychoanalysis.* This perpetual back and forth influenced his maturing years considerably. He will attest later that at this period "no analyst was a paediatrician, and no paediatrician was an analyst. For twenty to thirty years I was an isolated phenomenon" (Winnicott, 1962a, p. 172). A situation that would suit him, since he had been the only boy (isolated phenomenon) in the family.

Winnicott was accepted to start his training at the Institute of Psychoanalysis, London in 1927. In time he worked less as a paediatrician and increasingly more as a child psychoanalyst, but continued to keep an ardent interest in paediatrics with special emphasis on somatic disorders. It is equally his work with adult patients during their periods of deep regression that enriched his approach to the infant's precocious symptoms. He was qualified as an adult analyst in 1934 and child analyst in 1935. His work with children showed him that "something somewhere was not right": "Now, innumerable case histories showed me that the children who became disturbed, whether psycho-neurotic, psychotic, psycho-somatic or antisocial, showed difficulties in their emotional development in infancy, even as babies" (Winnicott, 1962a, p. 174). But he was not satisfied with the theoretical positions at that time, positions which privileged the Oedipus complex and instinctual conflicts to explain the process at work in the formation of neurotic symptoms.

The Melanie Klein years

It was James Strachey, his analyst, who advised him to undertake a control with Melanie Klein. "You will not get what Melanie Klein teaches in my analysis of you" (ibid., p. 173).

Melanie Klein settled in London in 1926, invited and supported by Ernest Jones, and she quickly surrounded herself with a dynamic and innovative group. The years 1928–1938 were perhaps the most productive years for the British Society. Winnicott notes: "It was during this period that my own psycho-analytic growth was making root and stem, and it might interest you therefore to hear from me something of the soil in which I had become planted" (ibid., p. 171). For ten years, a rich and authentic debate held sway at the British Society, and the progressive ideas of Melanie Klein proved a stimulation to all. For Winnicott, his encounter with Melanie Klein was of capital importance. His biographers delight in stressing that he met her shortly after the (premature) death of his mother. He was twenty-nine at the time and never mentions it in his souvenirs. It seems that he had hoped to start an analysis with her, but that she did not agree to it, having in mind that he could be the analyst of her own son, an analysis which she would control. Winnicott started the child's analysis but refused the control. Was this indiscipline the reason why she never forgave him? Be that as it may, Melanie Klein was working on a theory which threw light on the archaic world of the infant, placing the Oedipus complex and the development of the superego at a very early age. "I now learned psycho-analysis from Melanie Klein, and I found other teachers comparatively rigid. [...] This was difficult for me, because overnight I had changed from being a pioneer into being a student with a pioneer teacher" (Winnicott, 1962a, p. 173).

After a promising start, his relations with Melanie Klein quickly became stormy. He was one of the five controllers she recognised (Rodman, 2003). So at that time, curiously, he was considered a Kleinian but at the same time, he was never completely accepted by the Kleinian group. His biographers differ on the subject: was it he (as he will say himself) who distanced himself because his personal position was not accepted by his controller? Or sadly did he have to suffer his isolation from the group because of his "independence"? He was member of the Middle Group—the group of independents—at the time of the Great Controversy which shook the British Psycho-Analytical Society in 1940.

To have some idea of the violence of the dogmatic positions at the time, Winnicott relates the following anecdote: when he confided to his second analyst, Joan Rivière, his project to write a book on the importance of environment, that is, the mother's function, she told him: "If you do that, I'll change you into a frog!" "Of course, she didn't actually say that" he corrects later, "but that is the feeling I had". And I would add that he gives us the impression of a witch in a fairy tale.

The more time passed, the more Winnicott voiced his criticism of the theoretical positions of the Kleinian school, and the more Joan Rivière's attitude to him became hostile, to the point of humiliating him in public meetings (Kahr, 1996, p. 64). Be that as it may, Winnicott's relationship with Melanie Klein always remained a kind of "love–hate". He was in six year's control with her (1935–1941), and later he recommended Clare, his second wife, to choose her as analyst. The relationship between the two women seems to have been equally tumultuous.

It was from the Kleinian ideas of "internal reality", "depressive position", and "manic defence" that Winnicott developed part of his theory. However in spite of recognising all that he owed her, he quickly became very critical of certain of her developments. He first dissociated himself from her with regard to the importance of the environment. "She would never fully acknowledge that along with the dependence of early infancy is truly a period in which it is not possible to describe an infant without describing the mother whom the infant has not yet become able to separate from a 'self' (Winnicott, 1962a, p. 177)." "At the beginning, he continues, that which exists is a whole where the environment and the individual are indissociable".

This importance of the environment was never fully recognised by Melanie Klein. In a letter to her from 17th November 1952, Winnicott criticises a statement professed by one of her pupils the evening before: "One felt that if he were growing a daffodil he would think that he was making the daffodil out of a bulb instead of enabling the bulb to develop into a daffodil by good enough nurture" (Winnicott, 1987a, p. 35). This botanical metaphor is a striking example of what Winnicott meant, a meaning not always fully understood.

The Second World War

Then in the Second World War, Winnicott was appointed consultant psychiatrist for the Government Evacuation Scheme in Oxfordshire. This was a vast plan to evacuate young children from London and other big cities to protect them from the heavy bombing of the Blitz. From the very beginning, Winnicott had tried to stress that although this project protected children from physical danger, it endangered their psychic stability by separating them from their families for a period which could prove to be a very long one.[1] Some of these children were placed in families, others in children's homes, or hostels. And as it turned out, although the separation had been difficult for these children, the return home was even more so. Each half (children, parents) had to find themselves again, get to know each other again. For Winnicott, these, often dramatic, consequences corroborated his theories as to the importance of the environment.

He created a new concept to qualify the damage caused by this situation, which he called "deprivation", which could encompass an antisocial tendency, one aspect of which (but only one) could be juvenile delinquency. Once again, here Winnicott could be accused of a lack of precision which leads to great confusion. The term antisocial tendency is probably the most misleading of his corpus. Why does he choose such a term to describe what is for him a *normal* stage of development of the individual, a moment when fusion occurs between the two roots of instinctual impulses (aggressive and erotic), a moment which can become pathological when the individual has experienced deprivation?

At this moment, the antisocial tendency keeps psychic pain at bay, and the antisocial act represents a sign of hope, the hope of making good what went wrong before. The experience gained during these war years and those that followed enabled him to affirm that the treatment of antisocial tendencies was not psychoanalysis, but the recovery of the environment which was missing.

Describing a Children's Institute at Bicester, he makes fun of himself and his "smashing" interpretations:

> Rather quickly I learned that the therapy was being done in the institution by the walls and the roof; by the glass conservatory which provided a target for bricks, by the absurdly large baths for which an enormous amount of precious wartime coal had to be used up if the water was to reach up to the navel of the swimmers.
>
> The therapy was being done by the cook, by the regularity of the arrival of food on the table, by the warm enough and perhaps warmly coloured bedspreads, by the efforts of David to maintain order in spite of shortage of staff and a constant sense of the futility of it all. (Winnicott, 1984, p. 221)

This is one of the essential points that he learned at this time: "That psycho-analysis does not only consist of making the right interpretation at the right moment."

The Controversial Discussions

At this time, the British Psycho-Analytical Society was being rocked by the conflict between the Kleinians and the Anna-Freudians. This was the era of the Controversial Discussions. We could say that war was being waged there, as it was in the world. As we have seen, the years 1926–1938 were extremely productive for the Kleinian group and for the British Psycho-Analytical Society. Melanie Klein was undoubtedly the "queen" of the British Society. And it was during this period that Winnicott finished his training and was caught up in this intense intellectual whirlpool.

The arrival of the Freuds, who were generously welcomed in 1938, upset the balance. Almost at once, the positions of Melanie Klein and Anna Freud concerning the psycho-analysis of children and the concept of the construction of the internal world appeared very different.

And even if Melanie Klein had reigned the last ten years as "queen", Anna Freud was recognised as "crown princess". The Kleinians on one hand and the Anna-Freudians on the other began a series of hectic and violent debates on such theories as the period of the Oedipus complex, the formation of the superego, the nature of a child's psyche, not to mention the technical consequences resulting from the different theoretical positions. Tension was high, and the personal antagonism heated passions even more.

At this period in time, Winnicott was very busy far from London with his work in Oxfordshire. However he made a point of being present at the scientific sessions, although he played a very minor role during these "Controversies". He had only just qualified as a psychoanalyst and lacked the necessary authority to come to the fore. In addition he was sandwiched between Melanie Klein and Anna Freud. At the beginning he was considered a Kleinian, since he had been designated by Melanie Klein as supervisor. But at the same time, on one hand he dissociated himself from a certain number of essential theoretical points, and on the other he was terrorised by the manner which the partisans of Melanie Klein tended to dogmatise her theories (Winnicott, 1987a).

Brett Kahr quotes a personal communication from Charles Rycroft in his excellent biography on Winnicott (1996, p. 82). In this, he formulates the idea that, as in his youth, Winnicott found himself in the position of the younger brother with two older sisters, Melanie Klein and Anna Freud. So, just as he had earlier found a solution to the problem by going to Cambridge to become independent, he found an important place in what is called the Middle or Independent Group, where he was always a leading figure but refused to become the official head.

This group, comprising Michael Balint, John Bowlby, Margaret Little, Marion Milner, Charles Rycroft, etc. constituted a sort of intermediate group of freethinkers between the two main rival groups of Melanie Klein and Anna Freud (amongst the characteristics of the Independent Group we find the following: they all recognised and used certain Kleinian contributions; all worked on the importance of the environment, the absence of which brought about trauma; as well as the "setting" which was being talked about at that time, all emphasised the importance of the analytical "holding"; like Ferenczi, all thought in terms of splitting of the self and worked towards the reintegration of the split-off self).

The Middle Group

Finally the controversy ended with an agreement, which avoided a scission by creating two paths of training. The students in group A followed a training path which included Kleinian and Freudian ideas, those in group B followed a training path uniquely Freudian. However, in both cases, after a first control with an analyst in his own group, each student had to choose a second control within the independent group. This agreement officially kept the British Society intact, but the hatred continued in silence (as Joyce McDougall recounts). Some of Winnicott's published letters show how he was continually preoccupied by the way things were evolving and the ever-present danger of explosion (Winnicott, 1987a, pp. 71–74). So in 1954 he sent this letter to Melanie Klein, Anna Freud, and Sylvia Payne:

> Dear Miss Freud, Mrs Klein
>
> [...]
> I want to draw attention to the effect of the official grouping. I am thinking of the health of the British Psycho-Analytical Society and trying to look into the future.
> My suggestion is that it is not only true to say that the A and B groupings were essential ten years ago and that the adoption of these groupings saved the Society from splitting, but that it is also true that at the present time the reason for this arrangement has ceased, that is to say, there is no danger whatever of the expulsion of those who follow Miss Freud.

Neither is it true that either group is likely to walk out; the Society has now settled down like any Society to the fact that there are scientific differences which automatically clear up in the course of time just as other and new differences appear.

[...]

Incidentally, if we in the present try to set up rigid patterns we thereby create iconoclasts or claustrophobics (perhaps I am one of them) who can no more stand the falsity of a rigid system in psychology than they can tolerate it in religion.

In writing this letter I am concerned with the future and with the fact that any one of us may die. I consider it to be of absolutely vital importance to the future of the Society that both of yourselves shall break up the groupings in so far as they are official. No one can break them up except yourselves and you can only do this while you are alive. If it should happen that you should die, then the grouping which is officially recognised in the nomenclature will become absolutely rigid and it will be a generation or more before the Society can recover from this disaster which will be a clumping based not on science but on personalities or even I might say on politics since the original groupings were justifiable but defensive constructs.

I have no reason to think that I shall live longer than either of yourselves but I find the prospect of having to deal with the rigid groupings that would become automatically established at the death of either of yourselves one which appals me.

[...]

Speaking as Training Secretary over the past three years I can say that my task would have been easier had there been no official recognition of groupings and as far as I can see there would have been no difference at all in regard to the placing of candidates who usually express their preference for a close association with one or another of yourselves (i.e., if they know anything about it).

I am addressing this letter to yourselves and sending a copy to Dr Sylvia Payne.

Apart from this there is no-one who knows of this letter and I think this is of extreme importance because, should you decide to abolish the ideal of official recognition of the two groups, this idea should come from yourselves.

Yours sincerely,
D. W. Winnicott

Second marriage and the mature years

We must also remember that it was during the war period that Winnicott met Clare Britton, who was to become his second wife in 1952. The years that followed were marked by an intense activity and creativity. As well as his clinical work, Winnicott wrote continually, and gave many lectures to a variety of audiences. He took on considerable responsibility at the British Psycho-Analytical Society, of which he was the President from 1956–1959 and from 1965–1968.

These were years of great invention. His audience went far beyond the actual psycho-analytical realm. His radio talks at the BBC made him very popular. He loved to speak in front of a non-specialist public: social workers, teachers, nurses and medical students, mothers, the clergy. In each case, he adapted his vocabulary to suit his audience, avoiding any psycho-analytical jargon. This doubtless obliged him to adapt his thought in order to remain comprehensible. But for those who read them now, this has also left a strange mosaic of texts on identical themes. In spite of this intense activity, (according to Clare Winnicott) he found time to read, play the piano, appreciate art and poetry, and to create numerous "squiggles" (In fact we should say "squiggle game", a kind of drawing by two people. Winnicott used this technique to start a line of communication with infants during their first consultations. We will come to this later).

Clare Winnicott remembers that when she was away from home, she would find almost every morning in the post, a squiggle that he had sent her "because my part in all this was to enjoy and appreciate his productions, which I certainly did, but sometimes I could wish that there were not quite so many of them" (Clare Winnicott, 1965, p. 15). In her memoirs, she particularly stresses how her husband could make each day feel like a holiday.

The survival of the object

The heart condition that Winnicott was suffering from did not seem to affect his activity until 1968, the year he gave a lecture, the text of which was published as *The Use of an Object and Relating through Identifications* (1971f). We will refer to this text later, a text which is essential in the understanding of what Winnicott was working on his whole life, "perhaps the most difficult thing in human development", that is, how he perceives the object as external and not as a projective entity. It is what Winnicott calls the survival of the object. And because the object survives, it can be used. At the end of the lecture, Winnicott was literally slated by the three discutants, which prevented any discussion with the audience. This episode was evidently extremely painful for Winnicott, and when he returned to his hotel, he suffered a massive heart attack. He developed pulmonary complications and remained in hospital for six weeks. He returned to London, and although very weak, immediately began to rework his text.

He took up his activities again at a rate hardly that of a convalescent. He often mentioned the feeling of urgency at the approach of what he felt his imminent death. But he carried on with his clinical and teaching activities. On the evening of the 24th January, he was watching a comedy on the television with Clare, sitting on the floor as they used to, and they fell asleep. When she awoke, Clare realised that Donald had died in his sleep, sitting next to her. Shortly before this last day, at the insistence of his wife, he had begun work on his autobiography (Clare Winnicott, 1965, p. 8), which began with this prayer: *"O God, may I be alive when I die."*

His prayer was granted: he was living, working, loving, joyful, and planning projects until the end.

Note

1. Letter to the British Medical Journal, written in collaboration with John Bowlby and Emmanuel Miller, which asks the authorities to postpone the project, which they feel will bring about serious mental consequences for these children. Cited by Brett Kahr, 1996.

CHAPTER THREE

Transitional objects and transitional phenomena

The transitional object

We must give credit where credit's due. We will begin with Winnicott's famous article, which initially made him well known in France, first to psychoanalysts and later to the public as a whole: *Transitional objects and Transitional Phenomena* (1953).

The concept of the transitional object enjoyed staggering success, since every parent, everyone who cares for children knows the importance that a particular object can have for a child. This is the special object that we call in France a *"doudou"*. The phenomenon of attachment to a particular object generally appears at around six, eight, ten months and continues to an age which varies with each child. In *Peanuts*, the popular American comic, one of the little heroes, Linus, never lets go of his blanket, in spite of the jibes of the others: thumb in mouth, and holding the blanket in his free hand, he silently defends himself against the attacks of the bigger children.

Having become the *doudou*, or "noonoo", the transitional object could have become yet another object in psychoanalytical theory along with object *a*, the internal object or the object of drive. However in his texts Winnicott tries to avoid a possible confusion with the internal object in Melanie Klein's theory. He insists on the fact that the object he is describing (the transitional object) is a possession, but that it is not (from the infant's point of view) totally external. Today there is not a single radio or television program aimed at young parents which does not allude to the importance of this capital moment in the evolution of the young child, shown "externally" by his attachment to the corner of a blanket, a soft toy, etc. (*Le Monde*, 2008: "The children's clothing brand Orchestra offers the service 'Where is *doudou*?' for parents faced with the despair of their children. They even offer to find *doudous* from other brands. www.orchestra.fr").

These "transitional objects" are sold as such in certain shops. New parents recount how they buy two or three at once, to be sure that they don't "run out", because they often know from experience how the absence (loss) of this object can be a painful catastrophe for their child (and for themselves!). The so-called *doudous* are even given as gifts for the newborn baby. What happens to them? It's up to the infant to decide. Some of them will actually become transitional objects, others will simply become toys. And in many consultations with children, the subject of the *doudou* comes up inevitably: "Has she or he had a *doudou*?", "Until what age?", "How did he/she give it up?" Unless the questions come from the parents: "Is it normal that he/she hasn't got a *doudou*? Should we be worrying about it?" For the fact that there is a *doudou* reassures the parents, who feel less guilty about leaving their child.

The doudou *is not always a transitional object*

The weakening of this idea today is often due to the confusion between "transitional object" and "favourite object". The favourite object is a soother, that is, something calming and reassuring, which calms the anxiety felt before falling asleep for example. But the favourite object is not necessarily a transitional object, in the Winnicott sense, far from it. With the resulting quid pro quo.

We must say here that in the idea of "transitional object" it is not so much the "object" which is important—although as we shall see, its concretism is important—as the term "transitional". "It is not the object (thing) itself that I am referring to, says Winnicott, but how it is used" (Winnicott, 1953, p. 5). And the only person in the whole world who can decide is the child itself. It is the way that he or she uses a certain object which will give it, or not, its role as transitional object.

The third area

What Winnicott tried to define is, and I will quote his own words, "the visible part of the iceberg", what we, as outside observers, can perceive of an infinitely subtle and complex process which marks for the child the moment of separation from his or her mother and the construction of an "intermediate area", "an area that is not challenged, because no claim is made on its behalf except that it shall exist as an area of rest for the individual engaged in the perpetual human task of keeping inner and outer reality separate yet interrelated" (Winnicott, 1971a, p. 2).

"The object represents the infant's transition from a state of being merged with the mother to a state of being in relation to the mother as something outside and separate" (Winnicott, 1953, p. 14).

So what we could call the sad, true story of the *doudou* is an illustration of the way in which the work of Winnicott has been emptied of its incisive content because of its simplicity. For the popularity of the term *doudou* has created a misunderstanding of the true influence of the theory of transitional space. Of course Winnicott did not "discover" the particular use made of a certain object, he simply tried to elaborate a theory. Incidentally, as he says with his usual modesty:

> It is, of course, possible to see that this which may be described as intermediate area has found recognition in the work of philosophers. In theology it takes special shape [...]. It appears in full force in the work characteristic of the so-called metaphysical poets.
>
> [...]
>
> I have introduced the terms "transitional objects" and "transitional phenomena" for designation of the intermediate area of experience, between the thumb and the teddy bear, between oral erotism and the true object-relationship, between primary creative activity and projection of what has already been introjected, between primary unawareness of indebtedness, and the acknowledgement of indebtedness. (Winnicott, 1971a, pp. 1–2)

This intermediate area of experience, which is not questioned as to its belonging to internal or external reality, constitutes the greatest part of a small child's real life. In his work he will come to call this intermediate area, "the third area", "the potential space", the "area of rest", the "location of cultural experience".

A place for living

It is therefore all about a "space", a "place", and also a "process" which needs a certain amount of time to develop, time and space illustrating a particular and singular topography. This intermediate area is doubtless Winnicott's most important projection, but—and let's make no mistake here—it implies a concept of the psychic apparatus which differs radically from the theories in practice at the time.

But then if Winnicott had really been read, his work would have appeared scandalous. The French had followed the teachings of Jacques Lacan and Françoise Dolto, so this approach was more familiar to them, but in the British Society, split between the Anna-Freudians and the Kleinians at the time, the best way out was to pretend to understand without digging too deeply. Winnicott himself had always followed the Freud tradition. In 1954 he wrote to Harry Guntrip: "Any theories that I might have which are original are only valuable as growth of ordinary Freudian psychoanalytical theory" (1954c, p. 75). But this is not so sure. And as we have already mentioned, it would be wrong to classify him with the theorists of the object relationship, since by describing the process that unfolds with the composition of the transitional area, he really threw new light on the subject.

We note in passing that the last few years have seen the "rediscovery" of Winnicott, by both the English and the French. Was it the death of Clare Winnicott, the "gatekeeper", which encouraged a re-reading (a *new* reading) by a new generation of analysts, less influenced by the personality of the author and the anecdotes concerning his life?[1] We cannot tell. We would opt for a slow and progressive diminishing of the "resistance" against the revolutionary aspect of his conception of the psychic apparatus.

Winnicott wrote "Transitional objects and transitional phenomena, a study of the first non-me possession" in 1951. Surprised by the success of these new concepts and at the same time concerned by the quid pro quo it raised, he felt it necessary and useful to publish in 1971 a revised version of the article in his book *Playing and Reality*, a text entirely devoted to what he called the potential area. It was the opportunity for him to repeat that he was not referring so much to the object as to the use the infant might make of it.

The use of an object

The human baby makes a long journey from dependence to autonomy, and on the way he encounters the transitional object, a companion for the route, which he will not hesitate to leave behind and forget when the time comes. Because, as Winnicott says, we do not grieve its loss, it is not internal, and so the feeling it arouses will not necessarily lead to repression (1953, p. 13). It simply loses its significance.

The sequence usually begins with an activity relating to the body (the thumb, sucking. Renata Gaddini has proposed for this moment the term "precursor object"). Very quickly, the manipulation of an external object (external only for the observer, not for the baby, as Winnicott repeats) or mouthing activity accompanied by sounds (babbling) is associated with this auto-erotic activity. In the novel *Fault Lines* (2008) by Nancy Huston, the heroine Erra sings in such a sublime way that she bewitches all who hear her. But she sings without words, creating a never ending space with her listeners. At the end of the novel we learn that Erra is Ukrainian and was "stolen" by the Nazis, to be adopted by a loving and caring German family. In this family, she meets an older Polish child, who was also stolen and who teaches her Polish. At the end of the war, the Allies decide not to send her back to her mother— who had in fact been found—because the Ukraine had fallen into the hands of the "Reds". She is then given to a Canadian couple with rigid educational methods, who are pathologically cold. From then on we understand how no language can accompany her singing. Her voice is the language itself. This is how, by means of this song without words, she is continually creating a space for herself, to keep herself alive, as if she is returning to the first days spent with her mother.

Winnicott adds, "One may suppose that thinking, or fantasying, gets linked up with these functional experiences" (Winnicott, 1953, p. 4). So an "object" or "phenomenon" will gradually emerge for the infant, which might be a bundle of wool, the corner of a blanket or eiderdown, a word, a tune or a mannerism, which becomes vitally important to the infant at the time of going to sleep. The infant cannot do without it. But we cannot really say that he "loves" it. He uses it as a *material sensorial support in an activity where we could say that he is dreaming the world, at least his own world*. We note here that in English "wool gathering" can mean to have one's head in the clouds, but that literally it means to pick up wool, which is a transitional activity for many infants!

For Winnicott, this phenomenon is situated in the "intermediate area of primary madness", and he adds "we allow the infant this moment of madness". And he adds "the transitional object lies between the subjectively conceived and the objectively perceived." It is, as is frequently the case with Winnicott, "a paradox to be accepted, and tolerated, and respected, and for it not to be resolved" (Winnicott, 1953, p. 2). "It can be said that it is a matter between us and the baby that we will never ask the question: Did you conceive of this or was it presented to you from without? The important point is that no decision on this point is expected. The question is not to be formulated" (p. 12). So the transitional object is as important for what it is not as for what it is. At the same time its concretism is essential. It should be able to be manipulated during an activity involving as much muscular as oral erotism. It should be able to be cuddled as well as savagely attacked. And finally it must "survive" in the Winnicott sense, that is, stay the same. It has to be real, that is to say ready to be found so as to be created.

"This object will acquire enormous importance", says Winnicott, "The parents get to know its value and carry it round when travelling. The mother lets it get dirty and even smelly, knowing that by washing it she introduces a break in continuity in the infant's experience, a break that may destroy the meaning and value of the object to the infant" (Winnicott, 1953, p. 4). We have heard over and over again that the transitional object "symbolises" the mother. This is not completely true. We could say "a support which helps to represent". Octave Mannoni gave it the role of "pre-symbolic object" (Mannoni, 1977). It is already "in the place of". At the same time it is not the subject of a magic control, as an internal object could be, even if it is relatively accessible and not out of reach, as the real mother often is.

Later on, when the infant begins to use sounds, he or she could associate this transitional object with a particular sound. He will be on the way to symbolisation and gradually a word will replace the thing.

Use of illusion

Winnicott writes: "The transitional phenomena represent the early stages of the use of illusion, without which there is no meaning for the human being in the idea of a relationship with an object that is perceived by others as external to that" (Winnicott, 1953, p. 11). Paradoxically, as we have seen, *it is the refusal of the object which creates it*, that is to say as real, external. We most often misunderstand the true impact of this theory of transitional area, crucial to its elaboration, which numerous commentators have not hesitated to criticise. According to these critics, there was no need to introduce the idea of a potential space into the metapsychology. For them, the area envisaged by Winnicott is simply that of the internal world. But here lies a major quid pro quo.

We cannot understand what it is about if we neglect what the notion of "illusion" represents for Winnicott. As we noted before, during the course of the period of "indifferentiation", the infant is held physically and mentally by an environment, *which is not known by him because it goes without saying*. This environment allows the infant to experience omnipotence. That is, by adapting as much as possible to the expectations of the baby, the environment—the mother-environment—will give him what he needs at the right moment and right place. The infant then has the impression that he has created what in fact he has just found. The object is thus found and created in the same action. The infant will therefore have the illusion that a world exists which corresponds to his capacity to create it. For François Roustang, "the world comes to us as much as we come to the world" (Roustang, 1994).

The infant as creator of his world

At this moment, it is indispensable for the infant to see himself as the creator of his world, a world composed of subjective objects, a world that he feels is under his control. Winnicott addresses this wonderful phrase to the baby: "Come at the world creatively, create the world; it is only what you create that has meaning for you" (Winnicott, 1987b, p. 101). When he evokes the omnipotence of the newborn, it is not a *sentiment* of power he means to describe, but an *experience of omnipotence*. In any case, he insists on the fact that this period of *illusion* is fundamental. He does not confuse hallucination and illusion. With hallucination, there is no difference between object hallucination and lowering of tension. In illusion, on the contrary, an intermediate area is needed, because the object has to be there, waiting to be found. But it is only found by means of this intermediate area.

The found–created

This primary approach to the world follows us throughout our whole life. It will be our particular way of *"existing in the world"*, *"colouring the world"* (Roustang, 1994), and this is what is described by the expression "found–created". With the success of this "experienced omnipotence", the progressive and necessary passage from illusion to disillusion will occur in a non-disintegrating fashion. The illusion of appropriateness is necessary, indispensable, before disillusion can intervene. But experiencing disillusion is as fundamental as that of experiencing illusion. This process of adaptation, on condition that it is successful, is going to secure the infant in a feeling that Winnicott calls *going on being*. In this way we can understand that the inevitable failures of adaptation to the environment might have a *positive* value. They allow the object to be situated as *external*, *"not me"*, thus starting the process which consists of knowing a world because, precisely, it is missing. The infant will therefore go from a world that is only made up of "subjective objects" to the world of *the object seen as external*. The paradox here is that the process that created the object as an object (that is, something other than me) is at work *in the very act of refusal*. And the continuing movement from illusion to disillusion will constantly be at work in the establishment and maintenance of the transitional area.

"From waking to sleeping", writes Winnicott, "the child jumps from a perceived world to a self-created world. In between there is a need for all kinds of transitional phenomena—neutral territory" (Winnicott, 1950, p. 186). The transitional object that we have described is of course "relegated to limbo", but the transitional area will be needed throughout life, since the entire individual is constantly "engaged in the difficult task of linking internal reality and external reality to each other". This area of rest in which "all we need is for it to exist" is also what Winnicott calls the area of the formlessness, where the individual can "just be", and which will be available throughout life, a dreaming area that Winnicott was the first to theorise. It is neither an area of illusion nor an imaginary area. It is perhaps the place of our greatest truth, the place the nearest to our "deep reality", the place where we *live*.

We can illustrate this idea by quoting, for example, how certain painters have said that in the middle of their creation there is a mysterious space through which they can "enter" the painting, how they are caught up in it and pulled into it. They notice that they are in an area "neither inside nor outside", where the painting is a part of them and they form part of the painting. In the same way, this transitional—or intermediate—area also exists in the direct continuity of the play of the small child who is "captivated" in his playing.

Playing and reality

For Winnicott, playing is the most essential activity of the human being.[2] "The natural thing is playing", he writes, "and the highly sophisticated twentieth century phenomenon is psychoanalysis. It must be of value to the analyst to be constantly reminded not only of what is owed to Freud but also of what we owe to the natural and universal thing called playing" (Winnicott, 1968b). For playing has a place in the intermediate area "where we are most of the time in our experience of life". It is only by playing that we make our life a permanent experience. Playing can only take place if we have managed to preserve in ourselves the intermediate area which is, according to his expression, "the place where we truly live" and the place where we can communicate. This is why Winnicott always insists on the importance of the intermediate area as *a possible place of shared experience.* "Where are we", he asks, "when we are doing what in fact we do a great deal of our time, namely, enjoying ourselves? [...] Can we gain some advantage from the examination of this matter of the possible existence of a place for living that is not properly described by either of the terms 'inner' and 'outer'?" (Winnicott, 1971e, p. 106).

This idea, which was very revolutionary at the time, upsets many certainties. Firstly, it indicates that the human being could only relate to reality through the "found–created" (we can clearly find here what will reappear in Jacques Lacan's interpretations of Reality). What Winnicott means to say, and which is often disregarded by psycho-analysis, is that it is capital that we take into account the existence of an area where the capacity can develop to "apperceive" the world creatively, a buffer zone, between reality and fantasy.

We can compare this with the strange mental state we feel when we find ourselves in the transfer zones of an airport, those moments when we are neither in one country nor in another, on our way, not yet arrived, an in-between which can produce unexpected creativity, or where we can feel trapped by heavy, sterilising thought. In the same way—although we should consider things in a chronological order—the journey of an infant through *"doudou*-land" is not without shocks, and sudden stops at the wrong place. Sometimes this journey has not even taken place.

During an interview I had with two young parents who came to consult about their little three-year-old girl, I suddenly asked: "Has she got a *doudou*?" The father, who I could not imagine as having any analytical knowledge, replied immediately: "No, The *doudou* is Mummy!" This little anecdote illustrates perfectly what happens when an infant cannot detach from the "real" mother, because the "internal object" cannot be trusted.

So in what Winnicott calls the "psychopathology in the area of transitional phenomena", the question is raised of possible avatars for the construction of the transitional area. For it is by this passage through the constitution of the transitional area—which is only a stage, as we have seen—that the capacity for the infant to use this acquisition depends, an acquisition which depends on the qualities of the environment, and, in particular, of its capacity to remain constant. What in fact Winnicott is trying to outline is the process by which the capacity to live the world in a creative way is built up, a process which lies between too close a proximity to reality and the thrill of living in a purely imaginary or internal world.

The transitional object and addiction

Winnicott gives us many clinical examples, like the "string boy", the account of a meeting with a child who could only materialise the denial of separation by tying objects together with string. He had never been able to construct the world of the intermediate area, because he had had to deal with his mother's depression. Winnicott maintains that the small child can only use a transitional object when the internal object is alive, real, and sufficiently good (not too persecuting). "But this internal object [the transitional object] depends for its qualities on the existence and aliveness and behaviour of the external object" (Winnicott, 1953, p. 9). In a note added in 1969, Winnicott indicated that at adolescence, the "string child" had developed addiction, particularly to drugs, and asked whether "a researcher doing a study on this case of addiction, would have had the idea to take into account the psychopathology shown by this boy in the transitional object area".

This last small phrase at the end of the text opens vast perspectives. We must thank Joyce McDougall for continuing Winnicott's intuition in her development of "transitory objects", addictive objects which can be other human beings chosen to "take the place" of transitional objects (McDougall, 1995).

Today, the question of addiction is found in new areas, due to intensive exposure to television and video games. For some time now, we have been able to observe how numerous infants, who have been fed by mothers who were watching television at the same time as feeding their baby, could later on become very early "addicts" to the screen. Not that there is a connection between feeding experience and television, which would reflect a Pavlovian response that could be reduced to the equation: TV equals mother, therefore TV equals security. It's not that. It seems that we have to understand that the mother, lost in her contemplation of the television, gives the baby a breast (or the bottle), which cannot provide the function of the found–created object. It becomes what Kant calls "a thing in itself". From this moment on, the construction of a transitional area becomes more difficult, which could explain how later, the child has to continue to fill itself with a real object of substitution (bulimia, alcohol, addiction to the television, addiction to video games, compulsive sexuality).

One of my patients could not bear the separation from another person. The absence was unthinkable (in the real sense). He said: "I am included in my own loss." He was describing the failure of a transitional area. He compared his addiction to the other person to the necessity that certain homeless have of carrying around their paltry possessions in myriad bags which act for them as a barrier against the exterior, but which we can also think of as a transition—transition often odorous and reassuring—neither an inner area, nor an outer one.

Before Lily, the not-me object

After the death of her husband, Clare Winnicott entrusted to Anne Clancier and Jeannine Kalmanovich, the first translators of Winnicott's work, a letter he had written to her in 1950. In this letter he evokes what was for him the transitional object of his childhood:

> Last night I got something quite unexpected, through dreaming, out of what you said. Suddenly you joined up with the nearest thing I

could get to my transitional object: it was something I have always known about but I lost the memory of it; at this moment I became conscious of it. There was a very early doll called Lily belonging to my younger sister and I was fond of it, and very distressed when it fell and broke. After Lily I hated all dolls. But I always knew that before Lily there was something of my own. I knew retrospectively that it must have been a doll. But it had never occurred to me that it wasn't just like myself, a person that is to say it was a kind of other me and a not-me female. And part of me and yet not, and absolutely inseparable from me. I don't know what happened to it. (Clancier & Kalmanovich, 1987)

We could not say it any better: the fate of the transitional object is to be forgotten, but what always remains is the capacity to occupy this potential area. In any case, this transitional area of *experiencing* (Winnicott, 1953) should at best prove to be the space of the analytical cure (We will come to this aspect in the chapter relating to the cure).

Notes

1. The remarkable work of Jan Abram, *The Language of Winnicott*, shows the new interest the English have in his work. And as already mentioned, the publication of the biography by Brett Kahr is also an infinitely precious work (1996).
2. Sigmund Freud, in 1908 had already written that "the opposite of play is not what is serious but what is real". I imagine that Donald Winnicott was inspired by Freud's statement to call his book *Playing and Reality*.

CHAPTER FOUR

The importance of the environment

The absolute dependence of the newborn baby

As we have seen in Chapter One, one evening, after a Working Party at the British Psycho-analytical Society, and rather annoyed at what he had heard there, Winnicott exclaimed: "There is no such thing as a baby". This phrase gives rise to much confusion. What Winnicott wanted to point out was that "A baby is a complex phenomenon that includes the baby's potential plus the environment" (Winnicott, 1969, p. 253). Of course the baby is not a thing, he is already a human being, but he cannot keep himself alive. He therefore depends on someone else for his physical survival, and this dependence, which is absolute at the beginning, lays the foundation of his psychic life. In 1895 in "Project for a scientific psychology", Freud already talks of a newborn baby who feels instinctual tension and tries to discharge this tension which has gradually become unbearable pain, by the only corporal means at his disposal. He struggles and he cries. But the crying at this stage is simply an "economic process to attempt to reduce tension" (Freud, 1895 [1950a]). He is not calling. At this moment "someone"—*such a thing as someone*—comes, who will answer him. This solution is first and foremost the sign of an interpretation of the meaning of the cry. Freud, in "Project for

43

scientific psychology", uses in this respect the term *Angriff*, which can be translated as "interpretation", "intervention", or even "intrusion" (according to Monique Schneider).

To a certain extent, it is this solution that gives meaning to the corporal feeling that preceded it. So it is the answer that gives the crying its value as a call. What we could call the corporal memory is imprinted with the primary painful sensation and the response. The response may perhaps have nothing much to do with what motivated the crying. It is therefore violence on the infant, but "a necessary violence" (Castoriadis-Aulagnier, 2001), according to the wonderful expression of Piera Castoriadis-Aulagnier, since otherwise the infant will remain in a chaotic experience, unthinkable, impossible to transform.

The infant-environment

But what complicates matters is that the answer comes from another human being—a fellow creature, a *Nebenmensch*, to use Freud's expression—which registers *the relationship to the other at the same time as the emotional experience* which accompanied the relaxing of tension, that is, the feeling of satisfaction.

Let us get back to Winnicott. In "Playing: Creative activity and the search for the self" (Winnicott, 1971b, p. 53) he points out: "a description of the emotional development of the individual cannot be made entirely in terms of the individual, but that in certain areas, and this is one of them, perhaps the main one, the behaviour of the environment is part of the individual's own personal development and must therefore be included". And later he adds: "Whatever the degree of importance we may assign to environment, the individual remains, and makes sense of environment" (Winnicott, 1988, p. 99). The originality of Winnicott's approach lies between these two "poles". "The centre of gravity of the being does not start off in the individual. It is in the total set up" (Winnicott, 1952a, p. 99).

What Winnicott was at pains to emphasise was our implacable alienation to the Other, which is the very component of our humanity. He also wanted to oppose the Kleinian position current in England at that time, a position stating that we need only take into account what would be a fantasy world uniquely linked to the individual. At that moment, he explains, "*the outside world does not exist as such and the mental structure of the infant includes the experience he has of the mother, such as she is in his personal reality"*, which is to say including his relationship to paternal principle. What Winnicott says is that, from the start, a subject comes into the world "with an inherited potential", which only becomes a unit-status thanks to the *appropriate* environment which sustains the tendency of the newborn infant to develop himself at his own rate. What he describes as a unit-status is a subject that is capable of *indwelling, of thinking autonomously and living creatively*. It is only after the establishment of this "minimum base" that it is justifiable to talk of neurotic mechanisms. In other words, *we first have to be healthy to allow ourselves to be ill!* Winnicott does not actually question the Freudian theory of neuroses, he goes further upstream.

To illustrate this point, we could say that there is no point in trying to repair walls that are constantly cracking if we do not first take care of the base, that is to say, the foundations. So in the beginning we cannot speak of the individual without evoking the mother or the person in that position.

According to Winnicott, "In other words there is something here which people call primary identification. There is the beginning of everything, and it gives meaning to very simple words like *being*" (Winnicott, 1966, p. 11), primary identification, whose mysterious aspect is already found in Freud's works, who considered that it came "earlier than any object-cathexis" (Freud, 1923b).

From unintegration to integration

So as Winnicott states, in the beginning the infant is unintegrated most of the time. He perceives things that happen to his body, but he is not conscious that these feelings belong to him, because he has not yet achieved the differentiation between what comes from the inside and what comes from the outside. Winnicott even contends that instinctual movements can be perceived as being as external as a hit or a clap of thunder. The infant feels sensations, but he does not know that they are his. He can move his limbs, feel painful colic, feel peaceful in his body, hear familiar sounds, but cannot yet assemble this corporal experience in a unit. In "Primitive emotional development" (Winnicott, 1945a), Winnicott notes: "There are long stretches of time in a normal infant's life in which a baby does not mind whether he is in many bits or one whole being, or whether he lives in his mother's face or in his own body, provided that from time to time he comes together and feels something" (p. 150). This is how Winnicott imagines living in bits and pieces. The infant is completely where he feels and at the moment he feels (see Sigmund Freud's phrase: "Concentrated in his soul, in his molar's narrow hole", 1914c). In the same way, the infant is not conscious of the fact that he is the same individual who can be quiet in his cradle and who will be screaming with hunger later on. He cannot assemble these two feelings, feelings which are too different for him to be able to think of them as one unit. It is the same in many situations: between sleeping and waking, at each awakening, the infant must reconstruct the world; when he closes his eyes, the world disappears; when he opens them again the world reappears. He can thus create the world, repudiate it, and then create it again.

This is a trace of what we find in adults who shut their eyes in the face of danger, revealing at that moment apparently maladjusted behaviour, but not completely, since we all store in our memory a time when the world appeared and disappeared "at the flick of an eyelid". In Hal Ashby's film *Being There*, the hero, who has until then lived shut away watching films on the television all day, finds himself one fine day confronted by the world outside. His reflex is to press a button on the remote control he carries with him, thinking that by doing so, he will avoid a situation he considers dangerous. Of course this doesn't work! In the present day, the craze for "zapping" seems to me to reflect the same action: we fragment our life, perhaps thinking that it will be possible to reassemble it by means of something else (a programme, a film, a romance) which could last long enough.

For Winnicott, these mechanisms—normal in early infancy—are a sign of the immaturity of the "ego" (I put the word "ego" in inverted commas, as we have already seen and will see again the problem of the choice of words). He occasionally evokes the "ego-kernels" associated with partial functions (urinary, anal, epidermal, salivary, etc.— Françoise Dolto developed the same idea in France, in similar terms). Every one of these "kernels" is very strong, but as we have just seen, there is not yet any connection between them. What will become "I" is at this stage simply a sum of dispersed feelings not related to each other. This is a way to illustrate Freud's famous phrase: "*Wo es war, soll ich werden*" ("Where it was—in an impersonal way—the 'I' must happen").

Primary maternal preoccupation

In fact it is the way in which the environment reacts when it meets the needs of the id that marks the construction of a specific psychic reality. For, as Winnicott writes, "it is the ego-coverage of the mother that will prevent the infant from being annihilated or destroyed by the violence of his drives and to be able to assemble himself" (Winnicott, 1956, p. 300). This is what Donald Winnicott means by a "good enough mother": a mother who is capable of providing "coverage" for the "ego" developing in the infant she is caring for. She is able to assure this function thanks to the particular internal processes in the mother during the latter part of pregnancy and early post-natal life. This is what Winnicott calls "primary maternal preoccupation": a state of madness—healthy madness! A sort of heightened sensitivity that the mother feels towards the needs of her newborn baby. He suggests that: "A sufficiency of 'going on being' is only possible at the beginning if the mother is in this state that is a very real thing when the healthy mother is near the end of her pregnancy, and over a period of a few weeks following the baby's birth" (p. 303). This observation, which was a consequence of his clinical experience, showed once again a shrewd intuition of what modern research has confirmed (recent research has shown that a hormone, oxytocin, could play an important role. This hormone, which is present at the birth, continues to be produced by the mother during the caring for the newborn infant. But the hormone alone is not enough to establish the state of "primary maternal preoccupation").

It is this particular physical state—a state that must be respected and protected—which allows the mother, thanks to her identification to the baby, to provide "at the right moment" what is necessary. Let's be clear about this! Winnicott does not idealise mothering: "primary maternal preoccupation" is a kind of psychic "availability" which allows the mother to be "more or less" adapted, a state which occurs during the last weeks of pregnancy.

Pregnancy implies very different experiences. There is first what is called gestation, the period in developping the mother feels the foetus developing inside her, together with the physical transformation and somatic discomfort that pregnancy entails. Then there is everything this new identity implies, this "being a mother" which takes shape in her psyche, which mobilises her unconscious links to her maternal imago, to her own mother, to the baby's father, and which recapture her own experience as a newborn baby. And finally there is the internal dialogue that she undertakes with the imaginary baby, which takes up more and more space in her mind.

Recent and surprising studies seem to show that the picture of this imaginary baby is formed between the fourth and seventh month. Then during the following months, a quite unexpected phenomenon takes over: the mother endeavours to "undo" this image. In a sense, she starts to give up this baby, as if she were preparing for the arrival of the real baby she is soon going to meet. But this imaginary baby never totally disappears, of course, and it is often this baby that the infant sees in his mother's gaze.

Such observations give food for thought and infinite reflection on the forthcoming encounter and open a whole new perspective, particularly when the birth has been premature and has not given the future mother time to prepare for this encounter. Has not the mother herself been a baby once, with corresponding memories of herself as a baby? These souvenirs either help or hinder her in her role as mother (see Winnicott, 1966). Moreover, this special situation she finds herself in does not only depend on her mental health, it is also influenced by the environment. In his very personal way, Winnicott insists on the essential role played by the father, which allows the mother to become introverted and ego-centric for a short while.

Winnicott is often criticised for not taking the father into account enough in his theoretical approach to the subject. It is an unjustified criticism, since he maintains "When I speak of the mother, I include father" (Winnicott, 1962b, p. 64). And he stresses the important role of the father, not so much the father in reality, but the father who is inscribed in the psychic reality of the mother. This is an important question that will be dealt with at length in further work. In any case, for Winnicott, the father is not a kind of "duplication" of the mother—although, for him, certain fathers are really better mothers than their wives (1945b, Winnicott considers that fathers can also go through a particular phase at the birth of their child, but that they have fewer occasions to show it).

It is really more about a father—that is to say a man—whose psychic positions are different from those of the mother. In 2006, the Musée de l'Homme in Paris organised an exhibition entitled "The thousand and one ways to be born". Here we learned that in Normandy in the nineteenth century, the father used to wave his nightcap between his wife's thighs so that the "paternal scent" would encourage the birth of the child. *Odor di papa!!*

And what interests us here—that is, everything that happens in the early stage—is that Winnicott insists on the containing role of the father. We can imagine it thus: the mother "holds" the infant, and the father "contains" the whole situation. "The young mother", he writes, "needs protection and information, and she needs the best that medical science can offer in the way of bodily care, and prevention of avoidable accidents. She needs a doctor and a nurse whom she knows, and in whom she has confidence. She also needs the devotion of a husband, and satisfying sexual experiences" (Winnicott, 1986b, p. 127). He also insists strongly on the importance of there being someone who can assume this role, in the event that there is no father. We note that what in France is called "maternity leave" corresponds more or less to the period Winnicott attributes to the period of "primary maternal preoc-cupation". I say voluntarily more or less, because it is regrettable that the post-natal leave is so short. Mothers in general consider that it is not long enough. They are right. Society should allow them more time to emerge from this special period.

Winnicott compares this episode to a withdrawal, even dissociation. And, curiously, he notes that it leaves no trace. Mothers have trouble in remembering when they recovered from it, and, he adds, "I would go further and say that the memory mothers have of this state tends to become repressed."

Clinically, I have often noticed that a new pregnancy can recall the memory of a similar state, like waking up after a bout of sleepwalk-ing. We remember that "something has happened", without knowing exactly what. A young woman in her eighth month of pregnancy con-fided to me: "I feel worse and worse, I can't think any more", and when I suggested that it was perhaps a normal state of "primary maternal preoccupation", she exclaimed: "Oh yes, it was the same in my last two pregnancies, I had completely forgotten! And I know that it lasts about two months after the birth". So we must insist once more on the fact that "a woman must be healthy in order both to develop this state and to recover from it as the infant releases her" (Winnicott, 1956, p. 302). I stress the term "recover" and the expression "when the infant releases her" to show the dual movement perpetually in play during this rela-tionship. For example, the mother whose child has died before the end of this period (sudden cot death) would find herself in a serious pathological state and in great danger. On the contrary, the mother who cannot leave this special state and who keeps the baby in this period of illusion more than he needs does not allow him to develop a personal mental area, a "potential area", where the Other does not know every-thing about him.

Clinical results also describe cases where even if the mother is capa-ble of entering this very special state, the identification with her baby can take her back to the menace of primitive agony that she experienced herself as a baby. In such cases, the mother can feel her baby is a danger to herself, or she can feel herself such a danger for her baby that she pre-fers to keep her distance (this is related in Madeleine Chapsal's book, *Ce que m'a appris Françoise Dolto*, 1994).

This is also the theme of the film *Rosemary's Baby*, which describes a real case of puerperal psychosis, the hallucinating madness of a mother, where the genius of the director Roman Polanski gives the spectator the choice of deciding whether the infant is "really" the devil or simply a devil for his mother.

There are many different instances where the mother does not want to enter this state of "primary maternal preoccupation", where she may even resist it because her interests lie elsewhere. "In practice the result is that such women, having produced a child, but having missed the boat at the earliest stage, are faced with the task of making up for what has been missed. They have a long period in which they must closely adapt to their growing child's needs, and it is not certain that they can succeed in mending the early distortion" (Winnicott, 1956, p. 302). Winnicott may appear demanding and even reactionary (he wrote this in 1956 and he was thinking like a man of that time), but his position is a consequence of his theories. However these are not the only occasions where we find mothers who have difficulty in entering the state of "primary maternal preoccupation". We find cases of pregnancies at close intervals where often the mother has great difficulty in finding a place for the coming child in her psychic apparatus. For how can she reconcile a fusion with a young infant that is not entirely finished, and the arrival of another baby (even if it had been wanted)? How to reconcile "primary maternal preoccupation" with a new infant and "massive primary investment" in a child who is still dependent? How can she experience this state without giving the impression of "dropping" the older child? It is even more difficult when she herself has been such a baby.

At the end of his life, Winnicott stresses that fortunately someone other than the mother can assume this function, from the moment when it is possible to maintain continuity. He calls this operation *"the good enough environment"*. For what counts is that the line of life of the infant should be perturbed as little as possible (or not at all) by the reactions he has to implement to face environmental impingements. Winnicott constantly insists that it is the reactions that are important: each reaction that the baby is obliged to implement interrupts and perturbs what he calls a "continuity of being". The failures of the environment are such threats to the personal existence of self. "In the language of these considerations, the early building up of the ego is therefore silent. The first ego organisation comes from the experience of threats of annihilation which do not lead to annihilation and from which, repeatedly, there is recovery" (Winnicott, 1956, p. 304). "I refer to vital things like being held, being turned over, being put down and taken up, being handled, and of course being fed in a sensitive way which involves more than the satisfaction of an instinct" (Winnicott, 1962b, p. 70).

What Winnicott calls "primary maternal preoccupation" is also found in Bion's work, however he uses the term "maternal reverie". He believes that this particular mental state is a *function* of the mother that allows her to have an immediate understanding of what her baby feels. Such a state "predisposes" her to take into herself what he calls the "β-elements" of her baby, the equivalent of "the thing in itself" (Kant), which just needs to be evacuated for her to be able to "translate" and "transform" them into "α-elements" easily assimilated by the developing psyche of the infant. Generally the child's state of expectation—which Bion calls a "preconception"—can find a corresponding "response" in the environment, a response that in most cases manages to calm the infant in his state of distress. It is this response that gives a meaning to the corporal chaos felt by the infant.

Winnicott continues: "These are at first body needs, and they gradually become ego needs as a psychology emerges out of the imaginative elaboration of physical experience" (Winnicott, 1956, p. 304). It is clear that this phrase signifies first and foremost: *every experience, every thought is anchored in the body*. It is from this corporal experience—together with another, which is at this moment part of his "total experience"—that the infant gradually establishes the way to live in the world and his place in it.

The holding

"To be held, turned, put to bed, and of course fed"—this phrase sums up what Winnicott describes as the first three essential functions of the environment: holding, handling, object presenting.

First the holding. What is important to remember is that Winnicott is referring to a physical as well as psychic holding. In "The theory of the parent–infant relationship" (Winnicott, 1960a), he writes: "Along with this is the sense of personal identity which is essential for every human being, and which can *only become fact in each individual case because of good enough mothering* and environmental provision of the holding variety at the stages of immaturity." In other words, at that moment, this holding is part of the infant himself. Indeed, at this moment of "primary narcissism, the environment is holding the individual, whilst *at the same time* the individual knows of no environment and is at one with it" (Winnicott, 1954a, p. 283). This holding is the basis of what will progressively become "a self experience of being", "a capacity to prove one's self" (Winnicott, 1966). Winnicott is careful to describe what, for him, the holding is:

> I shall now attempt to describe some aspects of maternal care, and especially holding. In this paper the concept of holding is important, and a further development of the idea is necessary. The word is here used to introduce a full development of the theme contained in Freud's phrase '… when one considers that the infant—provided one includes with it the care it receives from its mother—does almost realise a psychical system of this kind' [Winnicott quotes here a phrase of Freud's in *Beyond the Pleasure Principle*, 1920g]. I refer to the actual state of the infant–mother relationship at the beginning when the infant has not separated out a self from the maternal care on which there exists absolute dependence in a psychological sense.
>
> At this stage the infant needs and in fact usually gets an environment provision which has certain characteristics:
>
> It meets physiological needs. Here physiology and psychology have not yet become distinct, or are only in the process of doing so; and
>
> It is reliable. But the environmental provision is not mechanically reliable. It is reliable in a way that implies the mother's empathy.

Holding:

- Protects from physiological insult.
- Takes account of the infant's skin sensitivity—touch, temperature, auditory sensitivity, visual sensitivity, sensitivity to falling (action of gravity) and of the infant's lack of knowledge of the existence of anything other than self.
- It includes the whole routine of care throughout the day and night, and it is not the same with any two infants because it is part of the infant, and no two infants are alike.
- Also it follows the minute day-to-day changes belonging to the infant's growth and development, both physical and psychological.

It should be noted that mothers who have it in them to provide good-enough care can be enabled to do better by being cared for themselves in a way that acknowledges the essential nature of their task. Mothers who do not have it in them to provide good-enough care cannot be made good enough by mere instruction.

Holding includes especially the physical holding of the infant, which is a form of loving. It is perhaps the only way in which a mother can show the infant her love. (Winnicott, 1960a, p. 48)

We can see that this is what every mother does spontaneously in caring for a baby. Let us go back to what Winnicott calls "the routine of care day and night". It is the monotony of the regular periodic return to the same experience that allows the infant to find markers by which his capacity to wait (and therefore begin to think) can be put in place. This means time, repetition, constancy, and the endless monotony of the same thing. Later on, we will not remember the mornings. We will only remember the day when something occurred which changed the experience.

Above all, we must not forget that it is not only about the technique of caring, not only about love, but a sort of astute adaptation by the mother due to her entering into this state of "primary maternal preoccupation" which we have been talking about. This seems a terrible demand on the person caring for the infant. But we must not forget that, for Winnicott, this almost total adapting lasts a very short time, for very quickly, the growing mental activity of the infant allows him to compensate for the deficiencies of the environment. We must not forget either that these ideas are part of a more global conception of the advent of the subject, since "the important thing is that *I am* means nothing unless *I* at the beginning *am along with another human being* who has not yet been differentiated off" (Winnicott, 1966, p. 48).

This holding ensured by the mother-environment is certainly physical, but also—and above all—psychic. The mother has her infant "on the brain", we could say. She dreams her child. And there is no worse "let down" than that where the mother, plunged into a depressive state, or grief, will carry on with the holding, but with no emotional presence. In this way, post-partum depression constitutes an obstacle to the establishment of "primary maternal preoccupation", with its share of consequences if no one can take over at that moment. In the early stages that the infant goes through, any psychic "disinvestments" by a mother, withdrawn into her own interior world of grief or depression will have fundamental repercussions, even if they are not noticed at the time. Clinical studies often show us unexpected cases of breakdown in otherwise brilliant young men and women. History taking allows us sometimes to find an episode of maternal depression that took place in the very early stages. Harry Guntrip recounts his analysis with Winnicott, who had to intervene to emphasise the difficulty of the analysand to put up with the silence of his analyst (Guntrip, 1975). "You feel the silence like an abandon", he told him, "The 'gap', it's not you who are forgetting your mother, it is your mother who forgets you. You have to remember your mother abandoning you in the transfer you are making on me." Harry Guntrip was in the habit of writing up all his sessions in order to maintain a link with his analyst between one session and the next, just as he had to "work hard to stay alive", as Winnicott says, but "to stay alive in his mother's mind." He adds, "You do not need to go to so much trouble to stay alive in our space, even when we are not together" (quoted by Guntrip, 1975). As Winnicott explains, this kind of ordeal can only be put in the past after the experience, in the *present* of the therapy, of the effective *presence* of an analyst capable of re-*presenting* this *holding*, metaphorically of course. We will come back to this essential question when we consider the course of the therapy.

The handling

The second important function of the environment—just as important as the first—is the handling, that is, the way in which the mother manipulates the body of her infant during the care she gives him. It is all those little gestures that accompany feeding, bathing, changing, dressing, as well as caressing, and skin contact. Here it is not a matter of technique, but the way the mother "presents" body and psyche to the infant (hers as much as the baby's). "The way a baby is handled is as significant as a language", says Joyce McDougall (personal communication), paraphrasing Lacan. For if at that moment the infant experiences disintegration, the mother feels reassembled. She looks at her baby and sees him—in her own image!—as a total individual, like a complete person. And what the baby sees in his mother's face is that she lets him live this totality by the way she handles him. It is by these means that the process of personalisation is carried out, that is habitation of the psyche-soma (which Winnicott calls *in-dwelling*).

The vocabulary of this experience may seem a little outdated, a little naïve, but we only have to look around to see people who have the air of feeling at one with their body and those who give the impression of having "borrowed" it. In fact, yes, they have borrowed a body that they do not truly inhabit. It is not about corporal technique such as sport, or dance, but something more subtle, which Winnicott calls "psychosomatic collusion", a way of "belonging to oneself".

Therefore it seems to me important to stress here that in the analytical literature devoted to Winnicott, there is a confusion—which should be avoided—between *holding* and *handling*, a confusion that leads to misinterpretation allowing certain analysts to justify physical contact with certain of their patients. Even if Margaret Little (1985) recounts how he has held her head or hands for hours, Winnicott does not recommend embracing patients—far from it! In other words *holding* is always metaphoric. Whereas *handling*, if the first care and attention have not allowed the individual to fully live within his body and to trace the limits of it, recognise its frontiers, if—to put it another way—he has not been able to leave the state of formlessness, then it is up to us, the analysts, to use the only means available to us, that is to say, language. It is the words of the analyst that will be a support, and not his gestures.

Object presenting

For the third essential function of the environment, *object presenting*, we must imagine a baby who has never had a feed. Winnicott writes:

> Hunger turns up and the baby is ready to conceive of something;
> out of need the baby is ready to create a source of satisfaction, but

there is no previous experience to show the baby what there is to expect.

If at this moment the mother places her breast where the baby is ready to expect something, and if plenty of time is allowed for the infant to feel round, with mouth and hands, and perhaps with a sense of smell, the baby "creates" just what is there to be found. The baby eventually gets the illusion that this real breast is exactly the thing that was created out of need, greed, and the first impulse of primitive loving. Sight, smell, and taste register somewhere, and after a while the baby may be creating something like the very breast that mother has to offer. (Winnicott, 1957a, p. 90)

The baby creates the world

This experience is repeated a thousand times until the time comes for weaning. Winnicott continues: "From this develops a belief that the world can contain what is wanted and needed, with the result that the baby has hope that there is a live relationship between inner reality and external reality" (ibid., p. 90). What Winnicott emphasises—which is very important—is that at this moment *there is no interchange between the mother and the infant*. Psychologically, we could say that the infant takes from the breast *that is part of him*, and the mother gives milk to an infant *that is part of herself*.

This is how the infant gradually acquires the conviction that reality exists and corresponds to his capacity to create. He is the "god who created his world"—an essential moment! It is important at this stage that the adaptation of the mother should allow the infant this first period of illusion and omnipotence, for, as we have already said, this omnipotence has to be experienced. An aspect too often misunderstood of what happens during this quasi exchange is that the infant must be able to feel that instead of being subjected to his needs, *he is active in the realisation of his desires*, and so he becomes the subject of his wish. In other words, it is not as much fulfilling the needs of the newborn infant, but *letting him create the object*. These are the "ego needs": the infant must believe that he changes the world while the world changes him. In this way, the next task of the mother, which is just as essential as the preceding one, will be to undertake a progressive "disillusionment", that is, she will introduce "failures of adaptation" in small doses, accompanying the growing mental capacity of the infant that allows him to make up for these minor deficiencies. There gradually forms within the infant a mental picture of the mother which remains alive for a certain lapse of time ("X hours, Z minutes, H seconds", as Winnicott says), a time which will become longer and longer.

A continuing process

It is in this lapse of time that the transitional area described in the preceding chapter is created and set up, a progression from total dependence to relative dependence, until the final construction of autonomy. This movement implies that the mother is gradually recognised as a separate person. Winnicott's vocabulary and grammatical construction—particularly his use of the present continuous as a noun—prove how much he considers this a process, a movement that is never completely finished. So we're talking about a subject continually emerging, and Winnicott was convinced that throughout an individual's lifetime, this process could always be reactivated, provided that environmental conditions were met. Unfortunately a similar idea, that the beginning of psychic life starts from the "good enough" adaptation of a facilitating environment, has equally brought a rash of numerous misunderstandings. When he spoke of "the ordinary devoted mother", there were many who thought he was asking mothers for perfect devotion, which caused a general outcry. By "devoted" we should understand rather that the mother (when she has this role, but it could also be assumed by someone else) "consecrates" and "vows" part of her time to her infant. It is important to give time to the human baby, from the moment he leaves his mother's lap to that of leaving the family fold. As we have said, the human body comes into the world in a state of physical prematuration, and at the same time a sort of psychic prematuration, which means that we must continue to carry him to allow him to progress in his maturation.

CHAPTER FIVE

The baby is a person

The inherited potential of the newborn

"The infant comes into the world with inherited potential provided always that it is accepted that the inherited potential of an infant cannot become an infant unless linked to maternal care" (Winnicott, 1960a, p. 37).

This phrase of Winnicott's, so often quoted, was not always evident to him. He recounted how, at the start of his career as paediatric consultant, he had "great difficulty in seeing a baby as a human at all" (Winnicott, 1967c, p. 569).

It is his later work as analyst with "borderline" and psychotic patients, which led him—quite unexpectedly and, as he said, "whether I like it or not"—to explore the very first stage in the life of the individual.

The preceding chapter tried to show how, for Winnicott, the essential role was played by the environment, a role he insisted on all his life. The question that follows on from the phrase quoted above could be the following: what is this famous "inherited potential" which has caused so much confusion?

In "New light on children's thinking", Winnicott lets his mind wander through the different meanings of the verb "to think". He juggles with the different expressions in English using the same verb but with different suffixes.

Thought is a mystery

It is almost impossible to translate the subtlety and humour contained in the English language.

Winnicott writes:

> I was thinking, you might have programmed your conference according to the ways the word is used. When I *think* what I have let myself in for I am appalled. First I find myself *thinking round* the subject, cunningly hoping to get away with it by exploiting a distraction. But then I find myself *thinking around* the meaning of the word "think". Then I start to *think up* a way of presenting the contribution that I want to make. Every now and again I *think* some words that had better remain unsaid and I make a mental note: next time *think* before you accept this sort of invitation! However it would be *unthinkable* to get out of my obligation by excusing myself on the ground of having flu or gout, so I plunge in, in spite of the poet's warning that to *think* is to be full of sorrow.
>
> There is no alternative; I must *think* this thing *out*, without hoping to *think it through*. Then I shall have to take whatever will be *thought* of my effort, and take it in good part. Afterwards, of course, I shall *think* of all the things I have not *thought of*. How much better to have *thought forward* and to have predicted your criticisms. (Winnicott, 1965. This article comes from a lecture given in 1964, which, in its original form, contained a certain number of additional notes with which Winnicott enhanced his presentation, and which he added by hand to the typed up manuscript)

Winnicott plays an enthralling game with the many possible nuances offered by his language.

As he notes, it is "still quite obscure" and only "coming from my observations as a paediatrician", but:

> I suppose one could look at each of these meanings of the word think and try to apply them to a child of one year.
>
> Think—recognise (belongs to various kinds of maturity).
> Think around—try cunningly to circumvent (1 year & animals).
> Think around—lovingly examine (6 months + or –).

Think up—creating in absence of one's muse (2 years & animals).

Think—not speak (5 years, latency).

Unthinkable—fear of superego (develops with superego formation).

Think—take a comprehensive view (develops meaning through life).

Think out—do deliberate mental dissection (ask Piaget).

Think through—complete limited thinking task (maturity).

Think of—verdict after due consideration (2 years + or –).

Think of—remember (earlier than 1 year).

Think of—recall (later than 1 year).

Think forward—predict consequences (very early).

—Winnicott, 1965, p. 152

Immediately we see that Winnicott goes much further than a simple play on words, and creates a distinction between the thought associated with an imaginative or fantasying idea of a corporal sensation, and a thought which is the expression of a protective and defensive mode of function, a game with the intellect.

An emerging sense of self

"It happens sometimes", writes Winnicott, that "the baby 'mothers' himself by means of understanding, understanding too much. It is *'cogito, ergo in mea potestate sum'*". This will be developed in one of his first major works, "New light on children's thinking" (Winnicott, 1965, p. 152).

In fact contemporary research, and the evolution of techniques of investigation, have largely confirmed Winnicott's intuition. The book by Daniel Stern, *The Interpersonal World of the Infant* (1985) has been a valuable tool for me in my reflection and the writing that I intended to carry out on this subject. It has been the missing link that has enabled me to read Winnicott in a different way, and to free it from a reading that is somewhat heavy going and—I must say—rather difficult to digest. However, and for reasons which remain a mystery for me, this fascinating, rigorous, and innovating work is still in many ways largely ignored by psychoanalysts. My interest in the book by Daniel Stern was aroused by François Roustang's reflection on this work in his book *Qu'est-ce que l'hypnose?* (1994) What I am going to put forward now is directly inspired by these two works.

Daniel Stern maintains that "for the whole of the first two months, the baby *actively constructs an emerging sense of self*". According to him, this operation requires us to "rethink the social experiences of the baby before the age of two months" (Stern, 1985). But this clearly refers to what Winnicott was working on his whole life: he tried to uncover and describe the emerging of "I" from a primary structure including the *inherited potential of the infant*, and that which he has been immersed in since birth, and with which, at the start, he is intimately merged. "Intimately merged" does not mean "mixed up", contrary to what we often hear. Winnicott certainly evokes a "fusion", but it must be remembered that fusion is a "blending of different, specific things into one". This definition demolishes the idea that there might exist an almost autistic period in each newborn infant.

The infant comes to the customs barrier (Winnicott, 1969), which is birth, accompanied by "a sum of inherited features and inborn tendencies toward growth and development" ("If we have a little furrow between our nose and mouth, it's the trace of the finger of the angel who put her finger there to tell you to be quiet and forget divine secrets." Jewish proverb). It seems he is already capable of intense intellectual activity. He perceives everything "with formidable acuity" (Roustang, 1994, p. 32). He recognises, is able to choose, to relate to, he experiences states of "quiet unintegration". Present-day researchers call these periods the times of "vigilant inactivity" or "calm awakening", moments when the infant is relaxed in his cradle, far from states of instinctive excitement. According to research, such instants are fleeting, they last about ten minutes in periods of three hours for a full-term baby, and a few minutes in one or two hours for prematures. These are moments "where the newborn babies are physically calm, vigilant, and appear to be interested in external events" (Stern, 1985), and, I will add, undoubtedly to internal events. It is these moments of "vigilant inactivity" that researchers take advantage of for their experiments. They use them as "temporal windows which allow them to ask the newborn babies questions and to find the answers from activities in progress" (Stern, 1985).

The ability to choose

The experiments show that from three days on, the infant is capable of showing particular interest in a pad dipped in his mother's milk: "The newborn infant cannot control his head well, and cannot keep it upright. But if we lie him on his back, so that the head is supported, the baby has enough control over it to be able to turn from left to right. The movement of the head allows us to answer the following question: can a newborn baby recognise the smell of his mother's milk? McFarlane (1975) laid three-day-old babies on their backs and placed a pad dipped in their mothers' milk on one side of their head. On the other side he placed a pad dipped in another mother's milk. The babies inevitably turned their head towards the pad which corresponded to their mother, irrespective of the side where it had been placed" (Stern, 1985).

Equally, we find that the infant is interested more particularly in the human voice than in other sounds of the same pitch and intensity:

> Newborn babies suck well. Their life depends on sucking, behaviour which is activated by muscles in voluntary control. Even when he is not feeding by sucking, the baby spends a lot of time sucking everything that is within reach, including his tongue. The sucking unrelated to feeding occurs during periods of alert inactivity, which makes a "good answer" possible. It is easy to teach a baby to suck in order to produce an event. All we need to do is to put in his mouth a dummy that has an electronic device inside the teat—a pressure transducer. This will control the start of a tape recorder or slide projector, so that the tape recorder does not stop or a new slide is shown on the screen when the baby sucks in a certain rhythm. In this way, the baby controls what he sees or hears by maintaining a certain sucking rhythm (Siqueland & DeLuca, 1969). The sucking was used to see if the babies were especially interested in the human voice, and whether they preferred it to other sounds with the same pitch and intensity. The rhythm of the sucking brought an affirmative answer to this question (Friedlander, 1970).
> (Stern, 1985)

And in the very broad range of human voices, he recognises and shows a special interest in that of his mother. There is, in parallel, something even more fascinating: amongst the voices of a certain number of women, he distinguishes those who speak the same language as his mother. This connection to the human voice, and more particularly to the mother's voice (and also now that of the father, since both future parents have been taught the importance of talking to the foetus) has been the starting point for the establishment of techniques such as haptonomy.

The creative perception of his world

But the human baby is not only "this little mammal capable of discerning the smell of maternal milk and the tones of the voice he has heard during his time in the uterus." From the beginning of his life he is capable of recognising in one mode what he has perceived in another. In premature babies, for example, all the sensorial systems already function: touch, kinesthesia, smell, taste, hearing. Only vision will be realised a little later. Except that it has been found that premature babies synchronise with difficulty the varying sensorial information that reaches them. These experiments, which date from the late seventies, are essential and give food for thought on the capacity of the child [*infans*] for creative perception of the world, which we dealt with in the previous chapter. The experiments of Meltzoff and Borton (1979) correctly set out the problem and what is involved. These two researchers "blindfolded three-week-old babies and gave them one or other of two different dummies to suck. One had a spherical teat and the other had several protrusions on the surface. After the babies had had time to feel one or other of the dummies in their mouth, it was removed and placed next to the other untried one. The blindfold was removed. After a rapid visual comparison, the babies looked more at the dummy that they had just had in their mouth." So the baby seems to be equipped to "deal with transmodal transfer of information" (Stern, 1985). These cognitive capacities are also found in the ability of the infant to correlate intensive light and intensive sound, sound patterns and time patterns, etc. But most of all, we can see a subtle correspondence between what the infant *sees* and what it *does*. A two-day-old baby mimics the expressions shown by the adult: smile, grimace, frowning, etc.

Gesture as language

This is, in my mind, the starting point of what Winnicott developed, in his own language, as *the idea of the face that reflects what is there to be seen*. "Psychotherapy", he writes, "is not making clever and apt interpretations; by and large it is a long term giving the patient back what the patient brings in" (Winnicott, 1967a). It is the same with a face that expresses something and a mouth that smiles; the six-week-old baby is inclined to pay more attention to this face than to an immobile one. But Daniel Stern writes; "when the sound that is actually produced is in contradiction with the movement observed on the lips, it is the visual information which, unexpectedly, takes precedent over the auditive" (Stern, 1985). In other words, *we understand what we see* and not what is said. Winnicott gives the example of one of the favourite lullabies of English babies, a little nursery rhyme that calms and delights them, but the words are hardly very pleasant for them.

> Rockabye baby on the treetops
> When the wind blows, the cradle will rock
> When the bough breaks, the cradle will fall,
> Down will come baby, cradle and all.

—Winnicott, 1947

But Winnicott remarks humorously that it is the mother who is relieved to be able to sing these words! We can experience this every day, which leads Winnicott to stress the fact that even if everything happens in a flow of language, it is the behaviour of the environment which is highly significant—above all since it is "saturated" with non-verbal significants. The infant then finds himself faced with the huge task of having to decode signals that are often incoherent, often contradictory, between the "gesture which says something" and the "word that he feels".

In fact we have emphasised these current experiments to show how they revealed the cognitive capacities of the baby. It must be said that, in this game of "Correspondances" (in the Baudelairian sense), an environment which is so incoherent and chaotic can only lead to failure, and that the infant facing such a danger of breakdown or collapse has no choice but to "think"—that is to say, to use his intellectual capacity—as a defence.

The activity of a baby

In fact Winnicott has always insisted on the "baby's own activity". The baby attempts to influence his world to transform it his way and according to his needs. Winnicott tells the baby: "Come at the world creatively, create the world; it is only what you create that has meaning for you" (Winnicott, 1968a, p. 89). And tells us that "even if the baby is born immature, he is not passive." In spite of his relative motive helplessness, he learns very quickly to develop ways of influencing his world. We saw previously how this is only effective in the way it can "translate-transform" the environment. And so to cry, at first an attempt to discharge too much tension, quickly becomes an appeal to another, "the human being" beside us—the exact translation of the *Nebenmensch* in German. And it is in this area—between need, asking-calling, and interpretation-response—in this implacable inadequacy between demand and response, that the mysterious chemistry of desire gradually comes into being. But we forget too often that the experience of satisfaction can prove traumatising for the infant.

The infant is in fact tricked by this satisfaction, especially if it happens too early, or too quickly, and if the effort made to obtain it has not allowed the baby to use all the psychomotor tension that is "bubbling" inside him. Of course he feels relieved of his uncomfortable tension, but at the same time, he has lost something that was "himself", and which at that particular moment was part of him. He *was* that sensation.

After this experience, the world has changed, the infant is *different* and the mother too is *different*. "There is a hole, where previously there was a full body of richness, something that was worth finding" says Winnicott (1954b). Because the moment that appetite is satiated, desire disappears and the infant finds himself satisfied but isolated in a world that has suddenly lost its savour. This situation does not last long and appetite returns, but the infant does not know this yet. He will have to experience this over and over again in a way that is sufficiently predict-able and identical for him to be able to "internalise" it. In any case, at that moment he finds himself facing a "breakdown" in the vital process that leads him to the other. This is how Winnicott helps us to under-stand the Kleinian expression "bad breast", which for a certain lapse of time the infant has no more desire for. So the ambivalence of the newborn baby is immediately in keeping with his relationship to the world, whatever we do. He feels the pleasure of satisfaction at the same time as the displeasure of having lost something that just before was part of him.

Hallucination and illusion

When the feeling of need returns later on, the infant will be able to begin to hallucinate his feeling of satisfaction, thanks to the memory traces which he has kept from the former experience. But hallucina-tion "doesn't fill an empty stomach"(!) and the arrival of a real breast (the milk provider) is the only thing that allows the infant to leave the hallucination for the illusion that *an outside world exists which corresponds to what he expects*. Then he loses this world again, and everything will start again, time after time until the constant repetition of the experience permits its internalisation, and the possibility for the baby to anticipate the feelings to come. It is during this phase that the necessary process of disillusionment will take place. *The object has to be missed.* It is this lack that the environment imposes on the infant, helping him to know more about a world, which at the same time he has to reject. According to Winnicott's conception of an infant's development, the refusal *"is part of the process of the creation of the 'objective' object."* The primary interest and function of this refusal is to bring about the creation of the *exteriority of the object*, to place it out of oneself. A gradual disadaptation is therefore absolutely indispensable. An object which is "too good" at this stage is hardly worth more than a hallucination, for they each compromise the distinctive construction of the interior and exterior.

The baby is in constant interaction

Of course at this stage, disillusionment goes hand in hand with the maturation of the infant, who little by little transforms "through good times and bad" an "average expectable environment" (Winnicott, 1969, p. 251) into "the perfect environment".

I hope I have shown how the complexity and fragility of this process, this perpetual act of modifying oneself as well as the world (given that it is clear that the world at that moment also includes the infant) shows how much "the infant is included as an actor in the universe he knows" (Roustang, 1994). I call the movement (coming from the self) that pushes the infant towards the world, to encounter the world, the "altering contact". The movement that he makes modifies himself, but must also modify the world for him. For the *baby is in constant interaction*. We have taken an incredibly long time to recognise this evidence.

Almost everyone now knows the famous experiment of the "still face" (an impassive face, an emotionless face. The following description is inspired by that recounted in his book by Daniel Stern, 1985). "Several mothers and their babies aged from six to twelve weeks, placed in different rooms, interact by means of a double closed circuit television. Each partner sees and hears in close up the image of the other by means of the appropriate visual contact. As long as the video presentation is live, this set-up allows the interaction to proceed normally: the babies look closely at their mothers, mouth open and relaxed, their eyes showing a multitude of signs of their interest. The first period of interaction is the control. It is recorded on a tape, then the tape that has recorded the mother is rewound and immediately shown again on the baby's screen. The second (recorded) passage is the experimental situation. Although the infants see and hear again exactly the same images as in the first situation—the same mother, the same gestures, the same show of affection—their response suddenly becomes dramatically different. In the experimental situation, the babies, who had been happy the instant before, now show signs of distress: they turn away from the image of their mother, frown, make faces, and fiddle with their clothes. And finally a control presentation shows that they were not simply tired out by the session itself. The distress shown by the subjects during the recorded passage had obviously been the result of a form of disagreement—or discord—with their mothers' reactions and their own."

So the baby cannot just remain a spectator. His perception of the world is linked to the relationship he has to it and the response he receives from it. He constantly tries to give it a form and to impart repetition and stability. It is the "endless repetition of the same thing" that gives him the possibility to construct an area of liberty, precisely thanks to the security that this monotony brings with it.

When the infant lives a body experience that is sensitive as well as cognitive, he is modified, he becomes something other than he was before. And "it is important for him that the environment should send back a message which also includes his own modification" (Roustang, 1994). When the baby has no possibility to react on his world, or when the world sends back something other than what is necessary for his needs, he is overcome by intolerable distress—these are the "primitive agonies" which Winnicott studied. Very early on, this distress is noticeable in the movement of the eyes turning away, avoiding our gaze and contact that we observe in infants who are stimulated in an inappropriate way and who take refuge in a parallel world. They withdraw from a relationship that plunges them into a sort of compliance-astonishment. This inappropriateness of the environment is called impingements by Winnicott and the only defence the infant has at his disposition against this is the isolation of the self. These are essential points that we shall come to in the following chapter.

Encountering the world

In other words, no infant comes to the world "like a poppy in a field of corn". He arrives in a universe that was there before him, a universe composed of other human beings, with their culture, their codes, and their language, a universe where he has his place. He comes from the desire of his parents, from their desire and their history, he finds himself "caught up" in this group, before he can even "configurate" it by his action. He will find his place at the junction of two genealogies, defined by the signifiers that preceded it, in the *transgenerational impact*, that is, the fantasy of his parents.

He has to deal straightaway with a mother who, in his psychic reality, is an "integral part" of him. As we have seen, this is how the baby, with a few tricks up his sleeve, finds himself facing the enormous task of encountering a world "both foreign and familiar, to be able to translate it to the actual terms of his existence" (Roustang, 1994).

Winnicott questions the fundamental paradox that the baby must find a specific place in a world that is beyond him, and where he belongs in spite of himself. Since for the baby, it is the immediate environment that "mediatises" the world. It is the "other beside me", the "human being beside me", which gives meaning to the corporal feeling that the baby experiences. It is the same "other beside me" who helps the baby to get through his translation and "transformation" (in the Bion sense). Therefore it is difficult to find a specific place because at first we think with the thought process of the other—this "little other" who is also the "big other" (Lacan), a trove of signifiers. If what builds a subject comes from the Other, then the meaning comes from the Other. From this we can see how everything must take place in an "interaction". What Winnicott describes is the subject coming to the crossing of three paths: that of the data which accompanied him when he came into the world; that of a corporal experience which needed to be transformed and translated by the thought process of the other "in order to become integrated"; and that of a relationship to the Other, the trove of signifiers. *The subjectivity is constructed in the relationship to the other.*

In Winnicott's terms, "First comes 'I' which includes 'everything else is not me'. Then comes 'I am, I exist, I gather experiences and enrich myself and have an introjective and projective interaction with the not-me, the actual world of shared reality. Add to this 'I am seen or understood to exist by someone'; and further, add to this 'I get back (as a face seen in a mirror) the evidence I need that I have been recognised as a being'" (Winnicott, 1962c, p. 56). For Winnicott is also working on the idea that there is a *self*, a primitive self, which exists well before the building of an ego. He thus proposes the establishment of a completely new topography, which will be the subject of the following chapters.

CHAPTER SIX

The self

In "Analysis terminable and interminable" (1937c), Freud called his metapsychology "our witch" (*Die Hexe*. He adds: "I had almost said: 'phantasying'" (ibid., p. 225)), and compared drives to "myths", "The theory of the instincts is to say our mythology. Instincts are mythical entities, magnificent in their indefiniteness" (Freud, 1933a). He was thus warning analysts against the danger of considering any theory to be true, whatever it might be.

Fifty years later, Octave Mannoni, takes up the same ideas in *Un commencement qui n'en finit pas* and points out that the pathology of the theory is not the error. "The pathology of theory", he writes, "is to think it is the truth" (Mannoni, 1980 [translated for this edition]). Extreme prudence is therefore necessary if we do not want it to slip into dogma. What I have called Winnicott's metapsychology in the preceding chapters is not exempt from this warning. His conception of a "real" and a "false" self is an undeniable bouleversement and can leave us perplexed; however it is this conception that led him to "think" his clinical cases. Even if Winnicott stresses that he is faithful to the topographical and structural theories of Freud, there is no doubt that his conception of the ego is different from that of the founder of psychoanalysis. It therefore seems futile to try to superpose the two theories, or

71

even to try and compare them too much. We simply have to think that is it *another perspective*, even if it uses words we are familiar with, and more or less understand the meaning of. But we must be careful! With Winnicott, one word can hide another!

Difficulty of vocabulary

The first complication comes from the choice made by James Strachey, when translating the work of Freud into English, to translate the *Ich* in German as *ego*, a subject pronoun in a dead language that cannot convey the lively German *Ich*, or the French *Je*.

Bruno Bettelheim deals with this question passionately in his work *Freud and Man's Soul* (1983):

> No word has greater and more intimate connotations than the pronoun "I". It is one of the most frequently used words in spoken language—and, more important, it is the most *personal* word. To mistranslate *Ich* as "ego" is to transform it into jargon that no longer conveys the personal commitment we make when we say "I" or "me"—not to mention our sub-conscious memories of the deep emotional experiences we had when, in infancy, we discovered ourselves as we learned to say "I". I do not know whether Freud was familiar with Ortega y Gasset's statement that to create a concept is to leave reality behind, but he was certainly aware of its truth and tried to avoid this danger as much as possible. In creating the concept of the *Ich*, he tied it to reality by using a term that made it practically impossible to leave reality behind. Reading or speaking about the "I" forces one to look at oneself introspectively. By contrast, an "ego" that uses clear-cut mechanisms, such as displacement and projection, to achieve its purpose in its struggle against the "id" is something that can be studied from the outside, by observing others. With this inappropriate and—as far as our emotional response to it is concerned—misleading translation, an introspective psychology is made into a behavioural one, which observes from the outside. Of course this is exactly the way in which Americans regard and use psychoanalysis. (p. 50)

In France the Commission Linguistique pour l'Unification du Vocabulaire Psychanalytique Français decided first of all to translate the German *Ich, Es,* and *Überich* as *Moi, Soi,* and *Surmoi.* After much debate, the term *Soi* was replaced by *Ça.* Winnicott's use of "self" in English captures something of the French *Soi,* which was abandoned.

And last but not least, the translations of Winnicott into French generally replace ego by "*moi*", which is also "me" in English, so we have to continually return to the English text, because Winnicott does not use the term "me" in the same circumstances as the term ego. We saw this in Chapter One. Incidentally, in 1962, in "Ego integration in child development" (Winnicott, 1962c, p. 56), he takes care to use the subject pronoun "I" [*je*]. This is therefore a brain teaser for us and it completely modifies our reading of Winnicott, for by systematically translating ego by *moi,* we overlook his discoveries and what is more, we fail to see what he was trying to introduce. In short, let us repeat again and again, sometimes the understanding of his texts is a real puzzle.

In Winnicott's work, the ego appears as a part of what he calls *the global self,* of which it is the principal organiser. It is a specific function of it and, even if Winnicott talks of "*primitive me*", this can only be formed from a primary or primordial self. In other words, Winnicott is perhaps trying to say that the self is what is the most difficult to perceive and attain, and what we show of ourselves to others—and what we show to ourselves—is our ego, our conscious me.

To feel real

It is very difficult to give a definition of what Winnicott calls the self, all the more so since he himself shows hesitation, even imprecision on this subject throughout his work. If we perceive what he means by this term—or sometimes what he doesn't mean—it becomes more complicated to express it. We are therefore going to try to *describe* it rather than to *define* it. In the first place, Winnicott puts the fact of "feeling real" at the heart of the feeling of self, and he will always associate this idea with the idea which motivated him throughout his life, which is that the essential thing is to live creatively. "Creativity, then, is the retention throughout life of something that belongs properly to infant experience; the ability to create the world" (Winnicott, 1970b, p. 40).

Furthermore, he states "Only the true self can be creative and only the true self can feel real" (ibid., p. 148),—even if it is difficult to say what we should understand by "real". On the other hand, the clinical experience teaches us that the existence of a "defensive self" mode generates a sentiment of unreality and/or a sentiment of futility. As Winnicott explains in his first rough drafts, deep down, the self "does no more than collect together the details of the experience of aliveness." It takes root in the "summation of sensori-motor aliveness." and comes from "the aliveness of the body tissues and the working of the body-functions" (ibid., pp. 148–149). It is what he also calls the "primitive self" which is rooted in the foetal life. So he places the origin of the self very early, well before birth, in the intro-uterine life. He stresses that there is an "age" for birth, and says clearly that pre-maturation like post-maturation can pose problems for the development of the self.

The pre-natal period

In other words, for him "The only question is at what age does a human being begin to experience? An ability on the part of the baby before birth to retain body memories is something which must be allowed for, since there is a certain amount of evidence that *from a date prior to birth nothing that a human being experiences is lost*" (Winnicott, 1988, p. 126).

With this statement, he shows himself to be a faithful Freudian, and at the same time an extremely modern precursor. Freud, in fact, writes in *Inhibitions, Symptoms and Anxiety*: "There is much more continuity between intra-uterine life and earliest infancy than the impressive caesura of the act of birth would have us believe" (Freud, 1926d). We find the same idea in Bion, who evokes the unborn parts of the personality. And we also find it with Françoise Dolto.

As Winnicott suggests:

> It is well known that babies have certain movements in the womb which at first are rather like the swimming movements of a fish. The very valuable activities of infants are well known to mothers who look for quickening at the sixth month; presumably sensations also start at some time or other; it is at any rate possible and indeed probable that there is a central organisation present which is ordinarily capable of noting these experiences. *I wish to postulate a state of being which is in fact the ordinary baby before birth as well as afterwards.* This state of being belongs to the infant and not to the observer. Continuity of being is health. If one takes the analogy of a bubble, one can say that if the pressure outside is adapted to the

pressure inside, then the bubble has a *continuity of existence* and if it were a human baby this would be called "being".

If on the other hand the pressure outside the bubble is greater or less than the pressure inside, then the bubble is engaged in a *reaction to impingement*. It changes in reaction to the environmental change, not from personal impulsive experience. In terms of the human animal this means that there is an interruption of being, and the place of being is taken by reaction to impingement. The impingement over, the reacting is no longer a fact, and there is a return to being. This seems to me to be a statement which not only can take us back to intra-uterine life without demanding a stretch of imagination but which can also be brought forward and applied usefully as an extreme simplification of very complex phenomena belonging to later life at any age. (Winnicott, 1988, p. 127)

Winnicott takes care here to clarify that he is anxious to "keep a rein on his imagination"; he takes the precautions necessary at that time, since with such ideas, he could of course have been taken for a crank. Now, more than thirty years later and thanks to technical progress (in particular the echography), we see that he was right, even if it is regrettable that this same technical progress has led to problems in excess, a "perpetual exploration", practically "tracking" the foetus. For today, just as the baby is an object of observation the minute he comes into the world, so are the movements, reactions, and life of the foetus not entirely protected in his mother's womb, but voluntarily revealed on a screen ("The echography kills the fantasy", comments an echographologist specialised in pathological pregnancies, and Monique Bidlowski talks of "catastrophic echographies").

The psychic adventure begins in the pre-natal period

However we regard this "visibility", it does seem established today that the psychic adventure starts for the baby in the prenatal period. A great number of experiments have shown how the foetus reacts vigorously to any modification in his environment, and to the emotions felt by the mother, emotions that generate hormonal transformations that are transmitted through the placenta. We know a little more today about the great complexity of these neuro-hormonal circuits: adrenaline, norepinephrine, serotonin, oxytocin, etc. And recent studies have shown that when the cardiac rhythm of the mother's heart accelerates from fear, there is only a *fraction of a second* before the heart of the foetus starts to beat at twice the speed.

There is one famous experiment, particularly cruel for mothers. It concerns the work of Dr Gerhardt Reinhold:

> We asked expectant mothers to lie down face down underneath an ultrasound machine for twenty to thirty minutes. We did not tell them that in this position, the baby is calm and also stops moving. Once the baby has stopped moving, we mention to the mother that he is no longer moving. The terror induced by this information was expected and intentional.
>
> A few seconds after the woman had learned that her baby was no longer moving, the baby itself, who was visible on the screen, began to move again. None of the foetuses we observed was in danger, but, as soon as he felt the distress of the mother, he began to kick vigorously. (Verny, 1981)

Françoise Dolto has also often encouraged the analysts in training with her to compare the organic pathology or atypical symptoms of an infant during the first nine months of life to what could have happened in the same month of pregnancy.

In our clinical work we meet patients whose psychic life has been affected by an experience of terror or grief suffered by the mother during her pregnancy. When they can manage to express in words what they feel, they talk of *a hole, a whiteness, the presence of something which is impossible to represent*, something which does not belong to them, but which is imprinted forever.

It seems certain that the complexity of the exchange between the mother and the foetus ensures that he *"engrams" even before birth*. Primary and corporal experience is engraved in a "memory" which we still know very little about, except that we cannot ignore it. So, for example, we see that the periods of Rapid Eye Movement (R.E.M.)— or paradoxical sleep—of a pregnant woman correspond to the periods of R.E.M. of her fœtus. Faced with this kind of "correspondence", the researchers today have formulated the hypothesis that such periods permit the transmission of data, philogenetics, and ontogenetics, since it is also during these periods that dreams occur—and why not dreams common to mother and child? If we take a step further, nothing prevents us from imagining that the same thing could occur later, in what is called the "maternal reverie" (Bion), a dreaming that helps the mother make sense of the chaotic experience of the little baby (We know that sleep is a moment of intense activity. Studies of cerebral waves have shown that it can be divided into different stages that follow each other regularly during the night. We can therefore compare "slow wave sleep" with "paradoxical sleep", the period during which our dreams take place. We have called this stage R.E.M. (Rapid Eye Movement), due to the rapid eye movements of the person dreaming. We also note that these same movements are characteristic of certain hypnotic states).

So we reiterate that Winnicott's remarks that life *in utero* is the start of the "continuing feeling of being" are once more confirmed. The foetus experiences there the permanence and constancy of a certain number of elements: a regular beating around the umbilical cord, a cord that the foetus can touch, a sonorous, odorous placenta, stable temperature, and ease of movement—the infant is "like a fish in water"—a sonic world with the constants of the mother's voice, the father's voice and those of the immediate family circle. As Winnicott underlines:

> The point of view that I am putting forward here is that, at full term, there is already a human being in the womb, one that is capable of having experiences and of accumulating body memories and even of organising defensive measures to deal with traumata (such as the interruption of continuity of being by reaction to the impingements from the environment in so far as it fails to adapt).
>
> According to this view foetuses at full term come to the birth process each with an individual capacity or lack of capacity for dealing with the great changeover from being unborn to born. (Winnicott, 1988, p. 143)

After being born and arriving in a world totally different, cold and unknown, the infant needs to create a reliable universe that is linked to the impulses of his needs, to find his marks and stability. As we have seen, this shows the importance of rhythm, repetition, monotony, and equally the importance of a supporting contact.

These suppositions were the hypotheses of Winnicott's work, a way of organising, of "thinking" his clinical experience. Even if the present-day observations seem for the most part to go in the same direction, it is important to remain prudent and vigilant. The most recent specialised approaches are really only new speculation.

A "pre-self" or a proto-self

There are today two different approaches to the subject: one consists of considering prenatal life to be the *primitive state initiating a going-on* which carries on in post-natal development. At that moment it is a "pre-natal me", which corresponds to the idea that a weak me, an immature me, a sort of pre-me already exists at the very beginning of life (This is the point of view developed by Heitor O'Dwyer de Macedo, 1994). The other presumes that there exist *psychic instances which are particularly linked to specific modalities of pre-natal life."* According to Antonio R. Damasio (1999), it is about proto-self: "My hypothesis is that the feeling of self has a pre-conscious biological precedent, the proto-self, and that the oldest and most simple manifestations of the self emerge when the mechanism which started the core conscience operates on this non conscious precursor."

"A specific group of neuronal structures can act as support for the representation of current corporal states of the first order which I call the proto-self and, in doing so, form the roots of the self. We are not conscious of the proto-self. Language is not part of the structure of the proto-self. The proto-self has no perceptive possibility and has no knowledge" (Damasio, 1999).

In other words, Antonio R. Damasio puts forward the hypothesis that the *period of foetal life is a particular and necessary time for itself*. Consequently a birth which takes place normally is not a trauma that has to be recovered from, but an experience which brings an end to a certain state, but only if this experience has had time to come to completion. Birth therefore becomes a passage from one place to another, an opening on a new world, a world that the infant will have to reinvent to deal with it.

It is this position that Winnicott defends in "Birth Memories, birth trauma and anxiety" (1949a), in reply to the work of Otto Rank on *The Trauma of Birth*. So for him there is no reason to consider anxiety as something primary. On the other hand, *what comes first is the "primitive self" that can only reply by isolating itself from an inadaptation* that makes it lose its boundaries, even for a very short while. In "The Human Nature", Winnicott declares that this experience is already one of the things the infant experiences in the womb. According to him, it is not about anxiety at this stage. To be able to feel anxiety is already the sign of an elaborate development.

The primitive self

Winnicott will maintain throughout his work that the primitive self existing in the very heart of the human being must remain inviolable, this secret part of ourselves that we can only reach in certain privileged moments. A patient once said to me: "It's as if there was a completely inaccessible part of me that I didn't know existed, and as if in that place I was also totally inaccessible."

To deal with this primitive self, Winnicott resorts to using the character Humpty Dumpty, from a much loved English nursery rhyme. Humpty Dumpty is a little egg-shaped person, with eyes, nose, and mouth, little arms and legs, balancing on a wall. He falls down and breaks into a thousand pieces, which of course is difficult to put together again. Winnicott explains that in the beginning that is what the self is like: formless, unstable, and defenceless. At the beginning it is a sum of experiences.

In "Ego distortion in terms of true and false self", he argues "It is an essential part of my theory that the true self does not become a living reality except as a result of the mother's repeated success in meeting the infant's spontaneous gesture [*The Spontaneous Gesture* is the title of a selection of the letters of D. W. Winnicott] or sensory hallucination" (Winnicott, 1960b, p. 145). He supposes that at a given moment a natural movement or instinctual motion will come from the true self. If at that moment this movement meets an appropriate gesture coming from the mother, the infant will enjoy the illusion of creation and omnipotence. He continues: "The true self has a spontaneity, and this has been joined up with the world's events" (ibid., p. 146). The infant has made a movement which has modified the world, at the same time his own modification comes back to him like an echo. Each successful experience reinforces what Winnicott calls the "sense of self". The mother's ability to adapt to her baby's needs facilitates the illusion of omnipotence. This strengthens the "sense of self".

As time goes by:

Every new period of living in which the true self has not been seriously interrupted results in a strengthening of the sense of being real, and with this goes a growing capacity on the part of the infant to tolerate two sets of phenomena. These are:

1. Breaks in continuity of true self living. (Here can be seen a way in which the birth process might be traumatic, as for instance when there is a delay without unconsciousness).
2. Reactive or false self experiences, related to the environment on a basis of compliance. (Ibid., p. 149).

We already know that these impingements are inevitable and, for Winnicott, all these little failures of adaptation are almost immediately repaired by the continuity of *holding*. Winnicott is clear about this: "integrable" impingements reinforce the "sense of self", whereas those which go beyond the integrative capacity of the infant—the "protective shield"—pose a problem. It is only the massive impingements that lead to the primitive agonies that he is referring to.

Impingement and reaction

So what happens when the environment does not give the infant the proper response that allows him to integrate an experience in the sense of a reinforcement of the self? What happens when the mother imposes her own gesture, that which she feels appropriate at that moment, instead of responding to the spontaneous gesture of the infant? What happens, for example, when the real breast arrives before the infant has had time to set up the temporal gap that separates his need and his satisfaction, a space to contain desire and the creation of the world? There then occurs what Winnicott calls an "impingement", an impingement on the mental space of the baby, which he must submit to.

Clinically, we very often find behind what Winnicott calls this compliance (a technical term used in medicine to account for the adaptive flexibility of an organ) of the infant, a temporary revolt that results in slight symptoms (such as problems in feeding, sleeping, skin ailments, respiratory symptoms), and which for the most part go unnoticed. For, at this early stage, the self can only "react" in the face of "intrusion". And while he is reacting, he cannot "be". "It may be pointed out that the most important thing is the trauma represented by the need to react. Reacting at this stage of human development means a temporary loss of identity. This gives an extreme sense of insecurity" (Winnicott, 1949a, pp. 183–184).

Splitting, dissociation, and breakdown

When we talk of intrusion or impingement in such situations, we immediately think of overdoing. Something has broken in and disturbed the
course of the "continuity of being". This is what is often called "primary
trauma". But it can just as well be void trauma. This is what happens
when *something that should have happened has not happened*. The impingement here is in fact an *absence*, a *lack*, and not a presence that ensures
richness. How then can we memorise something that has not happened
but which, by its lack and absence, has brought about a distortion in
the constructing of the psychic apparatus? This is one of the important
points, and if impingement has occurred at a very early stage, something has really happened, but this something has not been able to find
its place. This type of original trauma does not induce repression—since
there has not been representation, which is a condition of repression—
but succumbs to a dissociation, a splitting, a breakdown, with the cor-
relating setting up of corresponding defences. We see that the mother's
interpretation of the signs the infant makes to her constitutes from the
beginning the splitting of the subject. But we should not forget the
baby's own activity. Winnicott remarks that there is a built-in strain in
human life that enables in-dwelling, which allows the infant to go from
unintegration—which as we know is a state of tranquillity—to integration (This state of primary unintegration is sometimes described as the
state of primary narcissism). Unintegration is calm, it is disintegration
which is painful.

The incarnate subject

He will also describe an incarnate subject, a subject "which has a body".
But at the same time, he takes care to specify, in a letter to his translator (we will come to this letter at the end of the next chapter), that the
expression "corporal me" is not totally accurate, and is not a satisfactory translation of the idea of self. For even if we know that the psyche is anchored in the life of the body, we must not forget that we are
dealing with a human being inscribed in his relationship to the other,
mediator/interpreter of the corporal experience, a subject who comes
into the world with a certain cognitive baggage and a very personal
capacity to develop, a subject "who has a brain and can use it".

Once more it is the mother who is supposed to meet the "needs" of
the infant. It is by the repetition of such experiences of omnipotence that
the self begins to have a meaning. Progressively "the true self quickly

develops complexity, and relates external reality by natural processes, by such processes as develop in the individual infant in the course of time" (Winnicott, 1960b, p. 149). So the self finds its place, and then a membrane—the skin—defines the imaginary boundary between the inside and outside. Winnicott notes: "So the infant comes to have an inside and an outside, and a body scheme. In this way meaning comes to the function of intake and output; moreover it gradually becomes meaningful to postulate a personal or inner psychic reality for the infant" (Winnicott, 1960a, p. 45). He is equipped to treat all stimuli as projections and thus keep them within the sphere of his omnipotence.

It is only once it has arrived at this stage of evolution that the psyche has come to "live" —as we might say—in the soma and that the psychosomatic and individual life begins. Winnicott considers that this is the most important movement. At different times he will call it the "personalisation", "the psychosomatic collusion", or "the dwelling of the psyche in the body" (*in-dwelling*, 1960a, p. 45). In parallel he writes: "There are three processes which seem to me to start very early: 1) integration, 2) personalisation, 3) following these, the appreciation of time and space and other properties of reality—in short, realisation" (Winnicott, 1945a, p. 149).

It is the success of these processes that Winnicott calls "maturation". "The central self could be said to be the inherited potential which is experiencing a continuity of being, and acquiring in its own way and at its own speed a personal psychic reality and a personal body-scheme" (Winnicott, 1960a, p. 46).

The mirror role of the mother

And so comes the *"Sum, I am"* (Winnicott is playing with the meanings—Latin and English—of the word *sum*: in Latin *sum* means "I am"; whereas in English the word means "the sum" and more particularly in Winnicott's language, the "sum of experiences") concludes Winnicott. But he continues "I am seen or understood to exist by someone. I get back the evidence I need that I have been recognised as a being" (Winnicott, 1962c, p. 61). It is in the mother's gaze that the infant sees himself, in anticipation of his unit status. For at this stage he is still "living" in distinct parts ("It is a question whether the individual's ego-nuclei do, or do not add up to one", Winnicott, 1988, p. 118) but sees himself as a unit in his mother's face. Winnicott, inspired by Lacan—who himself was inspired by Wallon—thinks of the mother's face as a precursor of the mirror stage. The baby perceives his self in the mother's face, then in a mirror. For the mother looks at her baby, and what is expressed in her face is in direct relation to what she sees there. But what does she actually see when she looks at her baby? The ideal baby that she was carrying in her womb? The imaginary baby of her infancy? The baby she has seen in her own mother's face and tries to identify with? Or is it herself, in the role of mother that the eyes of her baby reflect? And if she sees nothing, because she is depressed or grieving, it is even worse (see Green, 2001). In the event that the face of the mother is not a mirror, the infant does not get back what he himself is giving, and, considering the importance of interactions that we saw in the preceding chapter, the world does not reflect the infant's own modification. Winnicott illustrated this type of disorder by referring to the paintings of Francis Bacon who continually painted deformed faces. He writes: "Francis Bacon is seeing himself in his mother's face, but with some twist in him or her that maddens both him and us" (Winnicott, 1967a, p. 114).

In the same way, François Truffaut's film *L'Amour en fuite* shows an adolescent Antoine Doisnel "searching" in the bathroom mirror, looking for his face and trying to make it fit with his name! "Antoine Doisnel, Antoine Doisnel, Antoine Doisnel …" he repeats *ad nauseam*.

It is what Lacan for his part places in the realm of the imaginary.

In keeping with this idea, Winnicott considers that a child born with a physical malformation can develop a healthy self perfectly well, a normal image, consistent with the way the mother has looked at him. For the infant, what exists is normal. He illustrates this idea with the case of little Iiro, a nine-year-old boy he met whilst in Finland. He published this case in *Therapeutic Consultations in Child Psychiatry* (1971g) and these observations were taken up again in *Psychoanalytic Explorations* (1970a).

Little Iiro

Iiro was a baby born with webbed hands. The doctors were amazed at his fierce determination to resist the often extremely painful operations that he himself asked for.

Winnicott, who spoke no more Finnish than the child spoke English, managed to establish contact with him by the "squiggle" technique.

What transpired from this was the need Iiro had to be loved "provided I am first of all accepted and loved *as I am*" (Winnicott, 1970a, p. 270), which is to say before the surgery, before the process of transforming and improving his condition. In other words, he did not want to give up what medicine could offer him, but it was important for him to be accepted just as he was, or rather as he put it "as I knew myself through knowing my own body before I found people saw me as abnormal: and they were right because, as I gradually came to see and understand, I am deformed" (p. 270).

In an interview with the mother, she revealed that she was also born with the same deformation, and that throughout all her pregnancies she had worried that she would transmit this deformation to her babies. Only Iiro was affected, and she began to reject and detest him, until the idea that the problem could be resolved by surgery caused her to change, and begin to love him, not for how he was but how he would become, if she was determined enough. And Iiro bore the pain of the operations so as to give his mother the gift of the infant he had seen reflected in her face.

So according to Winnicott, "They have a sense that something is wrong and that there is a dissociation in their personalities and they would like to be helped to reach unit status or a state of time–space integration in which there is one self containing everything instead of dissociated elements that exist in compartments, or are scattered around and left lying about" (Winnicott, 1971d, p. 65). Such a process leads to a "continuity of being" which becomes a "feeling of existing", a feeling of self that leads in the end to autonomy.

We will see that the way Winnicott considers things leads to a very original conception of the cure. It is no longer only a "rememorising" or "reconstruction"—as Freud was hoping—but perhaps for the first time a "complete experiment", so that something could happen which had not taken place, that something could be imprinted that in infancy could not have been. But for the moment, the infant has no other choice but to set up defence mechanisms, survival mechanisms, so as not to disintegrate, not to "lose his identity", not to dissolve in a world with no limits. The "false self" is one of these mechanisms. This false self is necessary for each one of us. It has a structural aspect.

CHAPTER SEVEN

The false self

The caretaker self

The first time that the term "false self" appears in Winnicott's work is in 1949, in *Mind and its Relation to the Psycho-Soma* (1949b), one of his fundamental texts. He borrows the term "caretaker self" from one of his patients (he refers to the therapy with this patient on numerous other occasions which, as he will repeat, gave him "a unique experience for a psychoanalyst").

Once again, it is his clinical experience that has led Winnicott to develop a new concept. "Our patients teach us these things [...] because everything that we say truly has been taught us yesterday" (Winnicott, 1963b, p. 182). But as far as the theory he tries to apply to it goes, it is only in 1960, in "Ego distortion in terms of true and false self" (Winnicott, 1960b) and in 1964 in "The concept of the false self" (1964b) that he develops with more precision the idea of the false self.

This idea of a false self seems at first rather absurd, to say the least. It is for that matter one of his most controversial projections, one which has received the most violent criticism and which above all has led to mis-interpretation. Because what can false self really mean? We find another typical example of the way Winnicott works. A new element appears in the clinical practice. He doesn't attempt to avoid it on the pretext that it does not correspond to a pre-existing theory. He accepts it, and then tries to conceptualise what has appeared, sometimes awkwardly, sometimes completely creatively, sometimes too hastily. We can of course reproach him for these inaccuracies, which are often the source of misunderstanding or defensive reactions by his readers. However, we must agree that there is a constantly evolving thought and an exceptional clinical exactitude. In fact his life's work revolved around this idea of a split-off self.

During the course of his work, once he had clarified his position, he called this moment alternately "pseudo-self", "nursing self", "defensive self", or "protective self". So why did he use the term false self at the beginning? I think that it is simply in opposition to the term "true self". Whereas, as we have seen, the true self tries to remain protected and even, as he says, "*incommunicado*" (Winnicott's term), the false self (according to Winnicott's initial terminology) is that which the individual wants to show us, which is in contact with the world, and which often "functions" perfectly well. Our everyday work shows us that there are a great many people who are clinically healthy, but for whom the dominant mood of their lives is insignificance and emptiness. They say "there is nothing inside", nothing behind the facade. They live in terror that someday someone will see that they are all pretence—and everything will collapse.

In a brief note, probably dated 1950 and published in *Psycho-Analytic Explorations* (1950s, p. 43), Winnicott gives a first explanation of what he calls false self: "The terms are used in description of a defensive organisation in which there is a premature taking over of the nursing functions of the mother, so that the infant or child adapts to the environment while at the same time protecting and hiding the true self, or the source of personal impulses" (ibid., p. 43). We recall what we studied in the preceding chapter and how Winnicott states that the true self is the source of spontaneous gesture, of creativity. The adaptation to the environment at this stage allows the infant to live an experience of omnipotence, a state of necessary illusion. The infant, by his needs, creates the world "as if by magic". He transforms his need into creativity.

However we must admit that Winnicott has considerably complicated our understanding of what he wants to say. In his key text on this subject, "Ego distortion in terms of true and false self" (1960b) he gives us a definition of what he calls the "differing degrees of the false self" (which is the term he used at that time). We find under

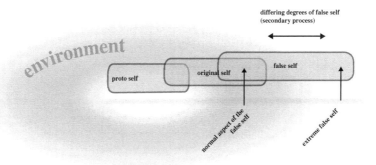

Figure 1. Formalisation of the concept of proto self, original self and false self.

the same heading both the result of a splitting of the personality where the subject is totally *identified* to this false self (this aspect seems very close to that which Hélène Deutsch conceptualised as "as if personality", but the false self that Winnicott envisaged is more of a defence mechanism against disintegration), as well as what we could call the "healthy" aspect of the false self, necessary to all of us, that is to say "much has gone to the individual's ability to forego omnipotence and the primary process in general" (1960b, p. 143). In fact this amalgam greatly hinders our comprehension.

I have tried to picture this new topology by means of a diagram. The third dimension is missing in the diagram, a depth of focus that would allow a better positioning of the area of transitional phenomena and, above all, the movement, since all this is happening permanently. In any case, I propose keeping the expression false self (it should be said that in ordinary language, it is this instance that we are referring to when we talk of false self) to describe a totally split-off personality and to use "modified self" to describe the *universal process which is a system of indispensable defence,* more or less rigid, depending on what the action of the environment will need to protect.

A mechanism of self-defence

Sandor Ferenczi had already remarked: "It is only in very early infancy or before the original splitting that one can really feel at one with oneself" (Ferenczi, 1982). He insists that the splitting-off is a defence mechanism. But when he talks of "split-off self", he surely presupposes the idea of a primitive true self. If we recall that Ferenczi was the analyst of Melanie Klein, we can imagine how this notion of a true self turned up in Winnicott's theories. The links were already forged. But it is difficult to know who has influenced Winnicott (apart from what he has always admitted he owes to Melanie Klein). He confesses in "D.W.W. on D.W.W.", "I never know what I've got out of glancing at Ferenczi, for instance, or glancing at a footnote to Freud" (Winnicott, 1967c, p. 579. Heitor O'Dwyer de Macedo, suggests in his latest book, 2008, that someone should take on the task of showing how much Winnicott owed to Ferenczi).

We must remember that at the very beginning, the inadaptation of the environment (when the environment adapts well at this early stage, it is neither perceived nor even registered, so that there is no feeling of dependence. But when the environment does not succeed in doing this, the failure is felt as an impingement) to do "what is necessary" provokes neither frustration nor anger. It causes an "unthinkable" anxiety, in the sense that it cannot be thought of, for it belongs to a time without thought. A defence mechanism arrives to combat this "unthinkable" anxiety, which Winnicott calls false self. We must insist here that it has the function of protecting the true self from unthinkable danger, the danger of being annihilated. In this light the false self seems an alternative to psychosis. In analysis with a child, for example, it is most important to have in mind the possibility of there being an organisation in false self, when facing a clinical picture which could be psychosis. This completely modifies the way we envisage the cure, and it also allows us to be more optimistic.

In his text "C. G. Jung, review of memories, dreams, reflexion" (1964c), Winnicott formulates the hypothesis that Jung avoided what was then called infantile schizophrenia by the construction of a false self. He further insists that this later allowed him to dispose of an exceptional faculty of insight, particularly concerning mentally divided patients. According to Winnicott, Jung spent his whole life in search of his true self, which sheds light on the course of his life, in particular the periods of dereliction he describes in his autobiography (Jung, 1963). But we must be clear: Jung's "self" is not Winnicott's "self"!

In this very early stage that Winnicott calls "primary maternal preoccupation", it seems that, by some mysterious means, the mother is in contact at times with her own self as a baby. By a method of identification, she communicates with her baby's self, which enables her to respond and adapt to his needs.

Every time that this mechanism fails (and we can be sure that it will sometimes fail), the baby can only comply with the consequent impingement. This compliance indicates an adaptation of the psychic area of the baby, a *protective* adaptation: this is the "modified self". In a play on words, we could say that it is a mechanism of "*self*"-defence. The modified self is therefore a protective construction that enables the baby to avoid disintegration, chaos, and madness.

The tree has two branches

In "Ego distortion in terms of true and false self" Winnicott compares the true self and false self to two main branches of the same tree, each one developing by itself, but each one hiding the other. "If you look around, you can see that in health this splitting of the self is an achievement of personal growth; in illness the split is a matter of a schism in the mind that can go to any depth, at its deepest it is labelled schizophrenia" (Winnicott, 1964b. I propose here, before taking it up again later, that Winnicott's "modified self" seems to me to be very close to what Lacan called the "*moi*", "*fonction imaginaire*" formed from "*précipité d'identifications*"). So it is only in really pathological formations that the rigidity of the false self is such that it blocks any access for the subject to his true self. In this instance, the individual is totally identified with this "role", like the actor who, having left the stage, remains in the character he played there. "There are actors who can only act, and who are completely at a loss when not in a role, and when not being appreciated or applauded (acknowledged as existing)" (Winnicott, 1960b, p. 150). The true self is not accessible for the individual who leads a life of appearances. As Winnicott reminds us, what we call the false self cannot experience real life nor feel "real". As an example, a patient said to me one day: "I advance masked and I lose myself". And Masud Khan, who was a long time in analysis with Winnicott, recounts how one day, Winnicott got down on all fours to look under the couch calling "Where are you? So where are you, Masud Khan?" Masud Khan describes how much this "acting" overwhelmed him, and how it made him conscious of the stalemate he was in, more than any verbal interpretation.

This mechanism is therefore an intermediate defence, somewhere between neurotic defence and psychotic defence. The organisation of a person "in a false self" protects from chaos and psychotic outbreak. It is a mechanism of "psychic survival". This is the aspect of the false self that is generally referred to, in spite of the repeated warnings of Winnicott, who tried to formalise degrees of the different aspects of false self. The difference is difficult to seize, since it is the type of description that we perceive as clinically exact, but which is written in the impossible style that renders Winnicott's work so difficult. We have to remember that when writing this first text (1960b), Winnicott only used the term false self, which led him to an occasionally unconvincing formalisation. Today, when we use the well-differentiated terms that he himself came to use later on, it is easier to define what he was trying to say.

So Winnicott makes a distinction between psychic organisations, depending on whether they are more or less rigid. Where they show a certain flexibility, we are obviously dealing with the "modified self", but access to the true self remains possible for the individual, at certain particular moments. On the other hand, the far more pathological situations are those where there is fear of annihilation of the self, if it is discovered. Winnicott will refer to this regarding the course to follow in the cure, as a warning to analysts who might take on treatment of personalities organised in "false self". They should weigh up the implication involved when they have to support the extreme dependence of the patient, or accept to be used. For, he remarks, it is at the moment when the false self "abandons its protective role in favour of the analyst" that any failure by the analyst at this point may lead to increased danger of suicide. This warning is even more important since it is related to the case of one of his patients who did commit suicide. Long afterwards he remarked that if he had better understood at that time more about what he now knew, "I think she and I could have enabled her to put off body death till old age took its toll" (Winnicott, 1963a, p. 93).

He finally comes to talk of the "modified self" as a structure constructed as an identifying response to the source data of the environment. He calls this "the healthy aspect of the false self", this organisation which is "the part of the subject which is linked to the world" (an expression borrowed from Patrick Avrane, 2007). In this definition we can recognise what Freud called the ego. This modified self ensures the continuity of being that protects the self and allows it to exist—and not to react, for Winnicott says that to react is to lose one's identity (during the reaction), which is extremely painful.

The tantalising mother and the split-off intellect

At one point in his articles devoted to the false self, Winnicott introduces the term "tantalising mother". The tantalising mother is a chaotic mother, someone who blows hot and cold, whose changing mood prevents the organisation of effective defences, someone who makes us feel so vulnerable, because she can become terribly seductive at will. He writes: "The mother here has as part of her illness a need to cause and to maintain a muddle in those who are in contact with her" (Winnicott, 1960b, p. 147). It is up to the infant to remain extremely vigilant and set up the necessary defence against what his senses perceive. In another text Winnicott extends this idea to the point of saying that the obsession certain adults have to continually listen to the weather forecast is surely a relic of this. We do meet people who feel it is important, even essential, to be prepared, to be continually adapted to "what is going to happen". For example, a young patient relates how her father used to telephone every night before coming home to find out what the atmosphere was like. He used to say to his daughters: "I want the weather forecast!" In those days we did not talk of a storm warning, the system telling us to be prepared for bad weather. He who is not prepared had better beware!

The split-off intellect

So as not to sink into chaos completely, in such an environment the infant holds on to a thought activity that tries to organise the chaos, to give a meaning to an experience which would otherwise not be integrable. It is quite a common process, but which is not generally recognised as leading to a false self.

An environment that is far too inadapted generally brings about the overgrowth of an intellectual activity dissociated from both the somatic and the psychic, which Winnicott calls the "split-off intellect", a mental function which becomes a "thing in itself" (Kant). He deals with this aspect of the false self in "Ego distortion in terms of true and false self" (Winnicott, 1960b, p. 144): "When a false self becomes organised in an individual who has a high intellectual potential there is a very strong tendency for the mind to become the location of the false self". With this article Winnicott again introduces a new term: "mind". He remarks in a letter to his French translator that "the term 'mind' can be deceptive, it is one of those concepts which are a consequence of the philosophical platform we come from. And this is surely not the same platform in England as in France [...] I would like the reader to be able to grasp the meaning of a concept which will lead naturally to the pathological formation of the split-off intellect" (Winnicott, 1971h).

Winnicott states that very early on, the mental activity of the infant allows him to make up for the inevitable failures of the environment. We have already seen that the infant is immediately active in the creation of his world. His capacity to think, even at its inception, transforms "a relative failure of adaptation into adaptive success". What progressively releases the mother from her need to be near perfect is the infant's understanding (he adds "One wonders if babies with a high IQ release their mothers earlier than the others"). This is why one of the tasks of a maternal function is to provide the gradual failure of adaptation, according to the growing ability of each newborn to compensate for relative failure by his mental activity or understanding. This is a very important point in Winnicott's metapsychological conception. Every human being comes into the world with a baggage and potential that, in the case of ordinary continuing of being, (the average environment which we can count on), allows him to construct a world that is situated at the crossroads of a body experience, the capacities of metabolisation of the somatic experience and the establishment of activities of thought, all of which take place in the linguistic and significant "bath" he is plunged into from the beginning (and this, even before he comes into the world).

In an environment which is both too misaligned and above all too unpredictable, in the face of considerable danger of breaking up, and primitive or dissecting agonies, "the intellectual function begins to take over" pathologically. Then an activity of thought is set up which functions in a perfect split-off, detached from corporal and emotional experience. The mental has replaced the environment, that is to say, *the function* of the environment. The child [*infans*] "models" his own environment by means of his intellect. *Thinking* is for him the only way he can keep himself together, to avoid madness. And afterwards it will prove extremely difficult to get rid of this activity of mentalization. This is how the artist and Zen master François Barbâtre comments on his experience of meditation: "Stop thinking, it makes the body hurt all over" (François Barbâtre, personal correspondence). Winnicott remarks astutely that, clinically, such a person may develop into one who is a "marvellously good mother to others, [...] or have almost magical healing properties because of an extreme capacity to make active adaptation to primitive needs" (Winnicott, 1960b).

In time, language appears as a very effective defence that allows us to talk for the sake of talking, so as not to face emptiness, lack, to keep distant from one's feelings. These are the people we meet who seem to live in a house of words.

The resulting clinical picture is distinctive in that we are easily taken in by it. After all, many individuals organised in this defensive mode remain that way their whole life, caught up in a successful academic and social life, without ever attaining their true emotional world. And why should they, particularly as society today happily favours this sort of disassociation? We live in a world of succeeding and "winning", where introspection is a dubious notion and boredom a condition that must be overcome at all cost. This is how we have children in consultation who have the busy schedule of a prime minister: "I'm afraid he/she is bored ...", say the parents. These children have no room for spare time, "to do nothing", just to be by themselves. And yet it is just these moments, this boredom, which often becomes a potential area of creativity.

We cannot stress enough how necessary these periods of emptiness and nothingness are, where we run the risk that a creative moment can emerge from the "formlessness". It seems to me that this "lost time" hardly exists any more, in a society where video games and television saturate the slightest empty space. Now it is the mobile phone that fills this function. This "filling-in" actually prevents access to distress hidden away in the background, an unsuspected distress (in this respect, the false self can be confused with "manic defence"), the distress of feeling an impostor, a charlatan. "I am really good at it", admitted a patient, "It's easy to wear the costume, but one day you will see that the king is bare".

It is also important to remember what Winnicott maintained his whole life. Every individual holds in hope that one day the environmental conditions will permit the correction of primitive failures. This implies that there is a latent capacity to regress and for this to happen, a defence must be organised from the start against the attacks felt by the self. This defence is the "modified self", that is, the "healthy" positive aspect of the false self. Winnicott is careful to describe what we are faced with most of the time at the beginning of psycho-analytical work with these modified personalities. For the question is, how can we recognise in analysis that we are dealing with a false self?

Winnicott remarks that what we notice very quickly is that there is an impossibility to communicate any sort of spontaneity in a lively, personal way. He describes the cure of a little girl in "Child analysis in the latency period" (Winnicott, 1958c). At every consultation she made pretty, organised, well constructed drawings which were completely defensive, to such an extent that Winnicott was bored throughout the sessions, which was an indication for him of what was happening. "The girl seemed to blot me out" (1958c, p. 139), he confides. In the same way, the patient whose cure is the object of his book *Holding and Interpretation: Fragment of an Analysis* (1986a) rattled off an elaborate, extremely circumspect, and tedious conversation.

We can perhaps mention in an aside that boredom can be a signal, not the creative boredom as mentioned above, but the boredom we feel on hearing a certain discourse. During a meeting he had with a group of clergymen, one of them asked Winnicott which criteria would enable them to know if they were able to help someone in distress, or whether it would be wiser to refer them to a psychiatrist or psychoanalyst. Winnicott replied: "If a person comes and talks to you and, listening to him, you feel he is boring you, then he is sick, and needs psychiatric treatment. But if he sustains your interest, no matter how grave his distress or conflict, then you can help him alright" (Khan, 1989, p. 1).

The missing subject

This is how a patient in false self will bring to the session an intelligent and intellectualised language, but absent from himself. The subject is not there. And if he has a certain psychoanalytical culture, he will be capable of building theoretical constructions, which are extremely interesting, which could even capture the interest of the analyst, if he lets himself be fooled. In fact such a patient tends to freeze the possibility of anything happening. He creates an area of conversation where he and his analyst find themselves paralysed. We can talk of "negative hypnosis" in such cases, a mechanism which creates a sort of anaesthetised thought. In Bionian terms, we could talk of "attacks on thought linking".

In his introduction to *Holding and Interpretation* (p. 15), Masud Khan, the faithful follower, evokes "it was boring-ness, not boredom. Boring-ness is an active existential stance, maintained through incessant mentation". "Tyrannically repetitive" is a good description of what is aggression in this attempt to dominate the analyst's capacity of thought, the aim being to keep the true self under cover. For this reason, it seems that there is no use analysing the false self. We could say it is as if a nanny had brought a child to the analyst, and then she and the analyst had discussed the problem of the child, without him ever being asked to play, draw, and talk. The analysis of the child can only really start when the nanny has left the room, when the child can show himself capable of being alone with the analyst and starting to play. For the false self, compliant and adapted, is always on the side of the analyst, with whom it happily collaborates, exposing exactly the right material that it thinks the analyst is expecting. We can use the term "collaborate" in all its meanings, for when Winnicott deals with the "compliance" of the false self, there is something of the feeling that the false self is a real "collaborator". This is how some people follow long, perfect cures without ever beginning to exist. As Winnicott recounts: "In one case of a man patient who had had a considerable amount of analysis before coming to me, my work really started with him when I made it clear to him that I recognised his non-existence. [...] When I had said that I recognised his non-existence, he felt that he had been communicated with for the first time" (Winnicott, 1960b, p. 151).

However we still have to work with the false self as long as we are not taken in by it. It is he (the false self) who comes to the first appointment with the analyst, who comes for a "trial" analysis to test the aptitude of the analyst to take on the protection of the self. And it is only when he has weighed up the reliability of the analyst that he will start to drop his guard (Winnicott does use the term "guardian self" in 1954, p. 254) but will be ready to take it up again if—and when—the analyst fails him, or lets him down (absence, holidays). At the beginning, cure is established very slowly, thanks to the "holding" made possible by the analytical mechanism. A patient once made the remark: "I felt held. And this feeling enabled me to lower my defences, to see what was in the centre." This is one of Winnicott's principal ideas, that the individual cannot indefinitely assume the charge of *being his own environment*.

"Because what the individual is all the time needing is to find someone else who will make real this 'good environment' concept, so that the individual may return to the dependent psyche-soma which forms the only place to live from" (Winnicott, 1949b, p. 247). It is about living: "the experience is of a non-purposive state, as one might say a sort of ticking over of the unintegrated personality" (Winnicott, 1971b, p. 55). The subject which has formed from the other's expectations can finally give up "being". This prompted a patient to say to him one day: "The only time I felt hope was when you told me that you could see no hope, and you continued with the analysis" (Winnicott, 1960b, p. 152).

Taking into account these remarks, we can understand how Winnicott very often warns young analysts of the danger of conducting an analysis with a false self. To begin with, the first danger, as we have seen, is not to "see" what is happening, and to analyse the false self. The patient and the analyst can therefore begin a never-ending process. Things seem to be going well. Each side feels intelligent, and everyone is pleased. This kind of work can even lead to an analytical formation, but all it will do is to build up the defences. Winnicott writes: "A principle might be enunciated, that in the false self area of our analytic practice we find we make more headway by recognition of the patient's non-existence than by a long-continued working with the patient on the basis of ego-defence mechanisms" (ibid., p. 152).

Regression to dependence

The second, more serious danger would be to embark on this kind of work and to be incapable of sustaining the state of massive dependence that the patient can find himself in. We must not underestimate the implication of the analyst at this moment, when he will be asked to be capable of spotting, accepting and supporting the state of total dependence that the patient needs to return to.

Margaret Little's account of her analysis with Winnicott (1985) is an extremely valuable account of what is "necessary" in certain difficult moments, where the risk for the patient is suicide or a serious somatic episode. We will tackle this subject in a later study, but Winnicott confessed that a single experience of this called on everything he possessed as a human being, as a psychoanalyst, and as a paediatrician.

> I have had to make a *personal* growth in the course of this treatment which was painful and which I would have gladly

avoided. In particular I have had to learn to examine my own technique whenever difficulties arose, and it has always turned out in the dozen or so resistance phases that the cause was in a counter-transference phenomenon which necessitated further self-analysis in the analyst. (Winnicott, 1954a, p. 280)

It takes much honesty and courage to admit such things! But the warning is important. The false self, which is a defence mechanism against the impingement (including the "void impingement") protects the primary self. Diversely, what we can call the "modified self", a necessary structure for all of us, is constructed by identifications and introjections in reaction to the "other". It is found in the "imagination", in the sense that Lacan gives to this term, because it is constructed by identifying what the environment expects. The modified self, the healthy aspect of the false self, would therefore be our conscious me, the only thing we can have access to, this "conscious me" which is the "ego" of the Anglo Saxons. Thus, in a nutshell: it is the ego that comes to the fore, whereas the self is there not to be found. "The sense of self comes on the basis of an unintegrated state which, however, by definition, is not observed and remembered by the individual, and which is lost unless observed and mirrored back by someone who is trusted and who justifies the trust and meets the dependence" (Winnicott, 1971b, p. 71). So someone is there to reflect him. For it is in the gaze of the mother that the infant anticipates his creation. But what the infant sees in his mother's eyes is not "him", but the ideal infant that the mother has in her head, the one she herself had perhaps seen in the eyes of her own mother, as we have already said. What the mother presents to the infant as a mirror is not what he "is", but what she expects him to be.

In any case, we can quite see how Winnicott got muddled with the analytical vocabulary of his time, and above all, how restricted he was by the way James Strachey had translated Freud's works for the English edition. The proof is that in the letter (already mentioned) written to his French translator on 19th January 1971 (Winnicott, 1971h)—five days before his death—Winnicott is still trying to make it clear to her what he means by "self":

I did wonder if I could write something out about this word, but of course as soon as I came to do it I found that there is much uncertainty even in my own mind about my meaning.

For me the self, which is not the ego, is the person who is me, who is only me, who has a totality based on the operation of the maturational process. At the same time the self has parts, and is in fact constituted of these parts.

[....]

The self finds itself naturally placed in the body, but may in certain circumstances become disassociated from the body in the eyes and facial expression of the mother and in the mirror which can come to represent the mother's face.

[...]

It is the self and the life of the self that alone makes sense of action or of living from the point of view of the individual who has grown so far and who is continuing to grow from dependence and immaturity towards independence, and the capacity to identify with mature love objects without loss of individual identity. (Ibid.)

Winnicott ends his letter by excusing himself for not having been able to help his translator any further, and insisting on the fact that one cannot really translate the term self as *ego* nor as *moi* (in French in the text). So dare we say je-me? It is just as difficult. In any case, at the end of his work, Winnicott will opt for the "I". So "*le moi* [according to Lacan, who aligns with Winnicott's view] is an imaginary function, even if at a certain level it determines the structuration of the Subject. It is as ambiguous as the object itself, of which it is in a way not only a stage, but also the identical correlate" (Lacan, 1988). How can we not be confused by these words? How can we not recognise here the modified self studied by Winnicott, formed at a moment when the individual and the environment are still undifferentiated, when the object is not yet constituted as such, at a moment when the inside and outside are not yet delineated. And as Lacan further states, in analysis we are only dealing with the "me". The "I", the Subject, is located nowhere, we never have access to it.

So on both sides of the English Channel, we must constantly be reminded that in analytical practice we have most often to deal with the "me", at any case at the start. When a patient comes to therapy, it is his "me" who addresses the analyst, and even, he believes, to the "me" of the analyst—ideas that we find in Winnicott, who thinks that it is the false self that comes to analysis.

Thus in London, echoing Lacan's development in Paris regarding the "mirror stage", Winnicott broadens the process and places it in an earlier period. The infant, he states, for a long time "does not feel whole", but "can live *as if whole*" both in the eyes of his mother, who sees her infant as a whole person, and in the gestures she makes in handling him. Compared with Lacan, who envisages an imaginary structuration of the subject from the specular image of the body itself, Winnicott always insists on the important function of the environment, which is what allows the infant to establish the connection between the psyche and the body. It is with an adequate handling that the natural force driving him towards personalisation leads to what Winnicott calls the indwelling, that is to say, the psyche living in the body.

But after all, Lacan and Winnicott were contemporaries. Each knew and followed the work of the other. The ideas circulated between London and Paris. And did not Winnicott declare: "So let's enjoy being ourselves and enjoy seeing what we do when we meet it in the works of others" (Winnicott, 1957b, p. 117).

It remains to say that Winnicott was more optimistic than Lacan, who maintained that we are only dealing with the ego, that we *never* have access to what is on the other side. However, on the other side of the Channel, Winnicott considered that up to the end of a life, there was always the possibility of change, "as long as the adequate environment is finally restored." And he even stated that the individual who had frozen the situation was searching for this condition his whole life.

CHAPTER EIGHT

Psycho-somatic illness and communication

An intellectual hyper-function

In the preceding chapter, we analysed a particular aspect of the false self, that which Winnicott calls "the pathological formation of the split-off intellect"—pathological being the important word here. In fact, as we have seen, the infant very quickly transforms an imperfect environment to an adequate environment by his capacity of thought. According to Winnicott, it is a normal process "taking part in the maintenance and re-creation of that environment" (Winnicott, 1988). Let us not forget that the infant "creates the world at the same time as he encounters it". By "pathological formation" Winnicott means an *intellectual hyper-functioning* set in place by the self as protection against *confusion* and *disorder*. And what he calls "psyche" in the expression "psyche-soma" is the "imaginative elaboration of somatic parts, feelings and functions" (Winnicott, 1949b, p. 243) elaboration which is an activity that is directly dependent on the reliability of the environment and its ability to permit a continuity of being.

With his description of this psychic activity, he distances himself from what influences our habitual way of seeing things, inherited from Cartesian philosophy. In fact he does not describe a body/mind duality, but a soma-psyche association, that can be perturbed, for example, when "This psychical elaboration of physiological functioning is quite different from the intellectual work which so easily becomes artificially a thing in itself and falsely a place where the psyche can lodge" (ibid., p. 243). We saw in the preceding chapter what he calls "the mind", a mental function which we know can be dissociated from both the soma and the psyche. Resorting to an intellectual hyperactivity is one of the possible methods of defence in the event that the environment is too inconstant. "As a more common result of the lesser degrees of tantalising infant care in the earliest stages we find *mental functioning becoming a thing in itself*, practically replacing the good mother and making her unnecessary. Clinically this can go along with *dependence* on the actual mother and a *false personal growth on a compliance basis*" (ibid., p. 245).

Jean and his mother came to see me, because, even if "nothing is really wrong", there is a sort of absence in their relationship, an emotional distance which only the mother complains about. Jean seems to have no questions. It seems he develops in an area he has defined safely and economically. He is an intelligent child, charming and open. Communication with him is very easy, conversational, far from any affectation. He is a very good pupil, poses absolutely no problem, practices his violin regularly and belongs to a sports club, which does not interest him, but he does his best—"does his best" is the right word, for Jean is not at all sporty. He is thin, gangly, and gets no pleasure at all from any physical activity. He likes to stay in his room, working, reading, and using his computer. I look at them both, mother and son, so similar: two people who are cerebral and intellectually brilliant but at the same time slightly stiff, slightly "awkward", as if they do not really live in their body.

Jean's father is also a brilliant academic. The conception of this child had been programmed by two people who admired each other, but refused to build a life as a couple. Time was passing for Madame X who was fast approaching the deadline for conceiving a child. Jean was born prematurely at seven and a half months. After a series of operations, an infection contracted when he left the incubator meant that it was one year before he could go home. Madame X explained how very helpless she felt when she finally held the baby in her arms. Since he had been fed by tubes, and been cared for all the time in a set rhythm, Jean showed complete passivity, silently waiting, to which the mother responded by the same kind of absence. Of course the infant had never been active in the process of creating his world. From the beginning his active role to encounter his mother was missing, which led to the situation where he could neither recognise her, nor position her as mother. Madame X was totally at a loss with this well-behaved, docile baby. She was however able to describe quite well the time when, according to her, the contact with her son started to become easier, which was approximately at the first stage of speech. This happened very early, but do we really need to say so? Listening to her, I thought that of course if the baby creates the mother as much as the mother dreams her baby, then the transitional area, the intervening area where they could have encountered each other was missing.

Jean was not psychotic. He was not "in another world", but he had built himself "as a false self", and it is this false self which was in contact with the world. He had spent several months between life and death in his incubator, the object of indispensable medical care, which was at the same time painful and intrusive. This false self had protected him during this experience of primitive agonies, and how real they were (real persecutions)! And as for his mother, from the start she had not been able to enfold this baby, and she was told he had little chance of surviving.

We can speculate ad infinitum and imagine what would have happened if things had been different. In other words, would Jean have had (or shown) sufficient liveliness to find his mother? It is difficult to say. On the other hand, what is clear is that Jean had used the resourcefulness of his intellect to remain assembled in the middle of the storm. He had avoided the break-up which would have led to psychosis. But there is no doubt that something was lacking in his emotional relationship. Someone was missing. Jean found himself helpless on the path to meet the other. And it was only after a long period of regression, sustained by his environment, that Jean was able to open up to the internal space that he had feared until then.

Another patient, a woman continually at the limit of anorexia, remarked: "I have the identity that the others have given me by looking at me. It's like a false personality. I feed my head and not my body. There is a dissociation between the two. Why can't I ever join one to the other, be a whole person?" The complaint that the patient in question had succeeded in formulating clearly that day can be understood as an illustration of what Winnicott affirms throughout his work.

There is in the human being a force that pushes to "personalisation" to "indwelling"—the psyche inhabiting the body—a force that constantly attempts to fill this splitting. One of the stages on the path to this "realisation" sometimes takes the form of a "psychosomatic illness".

Psychosomatic illness

Winnicott's conviction is that "in these terms, we can see that one of the aims of *psychosomatic illness* is to draw the psyche from the mind back to the original intimate association with the soma" (Winnicott, 1949b, p. 247)—in other words, draw the psyche back to its first association with the body. To put it another way, "One has to be able to see the *positive value of the somatic disturbance* in its work of counteracting a 'seduction' of the psyche into the mind" (p. 247). But it is a high price to pay: that of the somatic, physical illness, an illness that often absorbs a large part of one's vital energy. And yet Winnicott states that this illness, however disabling and vain it might appear, is already a sign of hope, hope and creativity at the same time. It is this creative part that the subject shows in his symptoms. It is a successful attempt to begin to resolve the conflict. For, like Winnicott, we cannot repeat often enough that to be ill is already a sign of "good health".

In this respect, Winnicott draws a parallel between the psychosomatic illness and what he calls elsewhere the "anti-social" tendency, which is also as much a sign of hope. But he specifies that it is not about "somatisation", nor "hysterical symptoms", nor "hypochondria". "It will be evident", he writes, "that I am making a distinction between the true psycho-somatic case and the almost universal clinical problem of functional involvement in emotional processes and mental conflicts I do not necessarily call my patient whose dysmenorrhoea is related to anal components in the genital organisation a psycho-somatic case, nor the man who must micturate urgently in certain circumstances. This is just life, and living" (Winnicott, 1964a, p. 106).

The physical disorders in themselves are not the illness. They are the expression of the dissociation of the subject, they are only the signifiers of an intrapsychic split. This split is extremely difficult to treat. "I have a desire to make it plain that *the forces at work in the patient are tremendously strong*", says Winnicott (p. 108). And he adds, what is more, the patient prides himself on his capacity to " ride two horses, one foot on each of two saddles, both reins in deft hands" (p. 108).

By putting it this way, Winnicott shows the fascination but also the annoyance and discouragement that can disconcert the doctor in the face of these sick people *who must not be cured*. In reality, the illness, in the medical sense of the term, is already a step towards greater integration. These patients multiply their consultations and visits to different doctors and specialists of fragments of their body. And the present-day medical organisation goes along with this fragmentation. "Patients with multiple dissociations also exploit the natural splits in the medical profession" (ibid., p. 111). Winnicott already noted that in his day "The more the treatments are specialised, the more the dissociation is maintained". The multiplication of the different sectors of the medical profession, each one treating the patient as if the problem were only physical, or each one treating an isolated aspect of the total problem, is a scenario for disintegration. It is a way of acting, but on another stage. Faced with this established fact, Winnicott emphasises how difficult the task is for the analyst. He must "allow time for time", and while waiting, the analyst remains powerless before the drama unfolding. Any attempt at interpretation would only result in the reinforcement of his intellectualised defence. The patient is only too happy to hear his analyst state something that he can integrate on an intellectual level, far from any emotion. After all, has he not protected himself this way all his life? There is here a seduction on the part of the analyst, seduction of the patient's intelligence. But it is what the subject has always known.

Nothing will really change in his symptoms. But he will be relieved to be able to say something about them. It's the well-known tale of the boy who is very happy after ten years' analysis. He still wets his bed, but at least now he knows why.

Winnicott believes that the only way out is to give the patient the time, the space, and the adequate place necessary. Thus the force that drives each human being to integration finally wins over the defence which was originally set up to protect the self, and which at present is exhausting its vitality. He writes in "Psychosomatic illness in its positive and negative aspects", "Psycho-somatic illness is the negative of a positive; [...]. The positive is the inherited tendency of each individual to achieve a unity of the psyche and the soma". "Psycho-somatic illness implies a split in the individual's personality, with weakness of the linkage between psyche and soma, or a split organised in the mind in defence against generalised persecution from the repudiated world" (1964a, p. 111). And he adds, "There remains in the individual ill person, however, a tendency *not* to lose altogether the psychosomatic linkage" (p. 112). This is the function of the psychosomatic illness. It is the *solution invented by the subject to recreate the linkage between psyche and soma.* "Here then is the positive value of somatic involvement" (p. 112). He sees there is no other possibility other than to create in analysis the conditions of regression which permit the return to the time before the moment when this dissociation took place. When the time and circumstances are favourable, the patient tends to recover from this dissociation. The integrative forces then push him to abandon his defence. But to be able to do so, there must be adequate psychic holding. As always, Winnicott insists on what is essential for him: the constitution of a psychic place where modifications are possible, the constitution of this place or return to the time before the traumatic situation, a time when all the self could do to avoid annihilation was to isolate itself.

An implicit communication with the subjective object

The logic of Winnicott's reasoning for the necessity to preserve the integrity of the self leads to one of his most famous paradoxes: he maintains that the *right not to communicate* must be absolutely respected. It is the principal theme of his paper "Communicating and not communicating leading to a study of certain opposites" (1963b), written in 1963. He was then sixty-seven.

"Starting from no fixed place I soon came, while preparing this paper for a foreign society, to staking a claim, to my surprise, to the right not to communicate. This was a protest from the very core of me to the frightening fantasy of *being infinitely exploited*. In another language this would be the fantasy of being eaten or swallowed up. In the language of this paper it is the *fantasy of being found*" (1963b, p. 179). The whole paper is one of his most important, in that it constitutes a kind of mesh holding the different aspects of his work together, a work whose principal themes are spread over numerous short papers at different times, with varying permutations often leading to confusion. In other words, this important progress comes from everything he had been developing up to then, like pieces of a puzzle that suddenly fall into place and create a whole.

In this paper, Winnicott emphasises what he calls "unconscious communication", dating from a preverbal time. This form of communication functions with a "subjective object"—which we must remember is an "object" that is not yet a non-me object—through "mutuality".

As we have seen, at the very beginning, the infant cannot recognise the environment, the mother-environment, as being outside himself. He has not yet been able to distinguish an inside from an outside. He is part of this environment, just as this environment is a part of him. "Even if it is repudiated", states Winnicott, "put over there, the object is still an aspect of the baby" (1969, p. 251). If we add to this that it is the response of the environment that gives a meaning to the somatic experience of the baby, we can understand that there is at that moment "a body and a mind for two people" (an expression of Joyce McDougall). By a relatively acceptable adaptation, the environment permits the setting up of the processes of symbolisation.

"We must assume that the babies of the world, past and present, have been and are born into a human environment that is good enough, that is, into one that is adaptive in just the right way, appropriately, according to the baby's need" (Winnicott, 1968a, p. 131). Needs and not wishes. "The word 'wish' is out of place as it belongs to sophistication that is not to be assumed at this stage of immaturity that is under consideration" (Winnicott, 1969, p. 251). In the term "need", implying necessity, Winnicott includes the necessary failure of the environment, a failure which lets the "objectification" of the object take place. For as we have seen, an object which is too good at that moment is not much better than a hallucination for the constitution of an inside and an outside. Once again, it is because the object is not there that makes it real. It is this which lets the infant go from the subjective object (that's me) to the objective object (that's not me). Before this stage, we can in no way speak of a relation to the object. We must remember that Winnicott is not a theoretician of the object relation, a misunderstanding doubtless due to the conclusions he came to on the transitional object. In so far as the object is subjective at this early stage, it is not necessary for it to be explicit to communicate with it. The communication with the mother-environment—not yet defined as external—will be subtle, to a degree.

When the adaptation and constancy are adequate, the infant communicates simply by continuing to develop in the personal process of maturation. But if the adaptation is insufficient or too unreliable, the infant will show his discontent by a somatic symptom, which will be either understood, recognised, or not. So underneath, the infant can only communicate his discontent, what is not right. But can we call this communication? The question needs to be posed, since it is this kind of question that faces the analyst in certain cures: he has to make sure he adopts the correct attitude opposite a patient in deep regression, a regression which plunges the patient into an implicit communication which asks to be recognised, that is, when the patient looks for *room in the psychic apparatus of the analyst*.

In the "normal" process of development, simple non-communication corresponds to the quiet moments of non-integration between mother and baby, moments when "just being" is enough. This non-communication is like resting (a state of vigilant inactivity). It is a state in its own right. It can transform into communication, and return as naturally to a state of non-communication. Thus the subject alternates between these two forms of being to the other and being to himself. Progressively the object is recognised as "not me", and it becomes then the object of drive attacks. Once the object is perceived objectively, there is a change in the means of communication, which becomes either explicit or silent. Here Winnicott introduces an unexpected element: at the same time as he claims there is the right not to communicate, he states that non-communication is a form of communication! As he explains, it is as if "I communicate that I am not communicating! For this to happen we as analysts must be ready for the signal 'I am not communicating', and be able to distinguish it from the distress signal associated with failure of communication" (Winnicott, 1963b, p. 179). For the individual enjoys using different ways of communicating, and tries to protect a self that does not communicate, the true core, living as an isolate. This is surely the key point in Winnicott's work. "Although healthy persons communicate and enjoy communicating, the other fact is equally true, that *each individual is an isolate, permanently non-communicating, permanently unknown, in fact unfound*" (p. 183). But he adds, "In life and living this hard fact is softened by the sharing that belongs to the whole range of cultural experience" (p. 184). And he concludes: "What is the answer? Shall we stop trying to understand human beings?"

"Active non-communication" is therefore a sign of maturity and results from a deliberate choice. It is part of health. In this respect, "non-communication" by a patient is a positive contribution.

The active silence

On the other hand, according to Winnicott, reactive non-communication relates to pathology. This form of non-communication can manifest itself as much by an active silence as by endless talk, which acts as a smoke screen. Silence is a form of non-communication which is typified by a silence of such violence that it becomes impenetrable both for the other person and for the individual himself. Here it is not the "capacity to be alone", in the sense of the isolation necessary for implicit communication, but an almost autistic withdrawal that for a brief moment denies the individual access to his internal world as well. Everything happens (as our patients tell us) as if there was no other psychic reality than that constituted by this effort of non-communication, not to communicate with the objective world, nor with their own subjective world.

This manifestation seems to be similar to that of the child who sulks. We all have patients who sulk, or who have been sulky children, and they all tell us about the tremendous effort they had to put into staying in this sulky state. They very quickly forgot why they were sulking, but what was important was to remain withdrawn from the world and from themselves. Some of them even say it was as if they were living in a place called "I am sulking" with at the same time the consequent hope that at least one person might know how to break the shell that isolated them from the world and from themselves. As Winnicott sums it up, "it is joy to be hidden, but disaster not to be found" (Winnicott, 1963b, p. 187).

The spate of words

Winnicott talks about the other facet of this same phenomenon—its most immediately disconcerting aspect, that of an "apparent" communication that comes from the split-off part representing the false self, and, in this case, it is the false self which is in reactive non-communication. There is an apparent communication, but it is a fake. The subject rattles off empty words. In everyday life, it is quite common to meet people whose incessant chatter fills all the space in the contact, leaving no room for a possible authentic communication and barring any access to the inner world, his own, as well as the other's. This mode of exchange—which is not one—establishes a type of relationship that tries to appear frank and warm, but which, if we look closely, is simply founded on pretence. During the obviously limited session time of the cure, silence is generally felt to be useless, like lost time and, often, even as something dangerous and persecutory. It is important for this type of patient to completely fill all the sound space to leave no possible place for the emergence of an internal reality which they do not wish to know.

Even so, this deceptive communication is never completely felt to be real. As Winnicott points out, "it is not a true communication because it does not involve the core of the self, that which could be called the true self" (Winnicott, 1963b, p. 187).

This manner of seeing things may seem to be the opposite of the "tell all" of psychoanalysis—"Say whatever comes into your mind"—and the rule of free association. But it can happen that language, an apparent communication, can be the best of all defences. What Lacan called *"lalangue"* is the exact opposite of this kind of empty speech which can go on endlessly, from session to session. We know that this is why he proposed that the analytic hour could be of variable duration. The signifying scansion was intended in practice to be a way for the analyst to signal that he is not fooled by this form of speech. In his own language, Winnicott likewise indicated that "it is only too easy for an analysis (where there is a hidden schizoid element in the patient's personality) to become an infinitely prolonged collusion of the analyst with the patient's negation of non-communication" (Winnicott, 1963b, p. 187). But he wonders "does our technique allow for the patient to communicate that he or she is not communicating?" (p. 190). Maybe not, and maybe it was to compensate for this inadequate technique that Lacan established in practice a way of terminating the session regardless of its length. It remains to say that this innovation was misused—and primarily by Lacan himself.

So that communication can be recognised as a form of non-communication, Winnicott writes, "For this to happen we as analysts must be ready for the signal 'I am not communicating', and be able to distinguish it from the distress signal associated with failure of communication" (ibid., p. 190). Some of our patients need, really need to return to the core of the "primary creativity", and must be able to find it in the cure. This means that in a session they must be able to experience a silent or secret communication with subjective objects and gain in terms of feeling real.

To accomplish silence

When such moments occur in patients who have always used speech as a defence, a mask, the analyst must allow this experience to unfold in its entirety without intervening or intruding in any way. In this kind of essential episode, episodes which only occur in periods of deep regression, the slightest manifestation by the analyst, even a clearing of the throat, runs the risk of creating an impingement and interrupting the current process. This is why the silence which the patient can finally bring to the cure without risk can be considered as an outcome. It is perhaps in these moments that he is able to be alone for the first time, but "alone" only in the Winnicott sense, in "the presence of someone else", alone in the presence of a non-intervening, non-intrusive other, who nevertheless is holding the situation. In other words, it is about "being isolated without being cut off from the world".

This way of regarding the space of the cure, this withdrawal of the analyst at the moment he becomes a subjective object, opens several paths. Winnicott puts forward the idea that "perhaps the answer might come from the mothers who do not communicate (in the usual sense) with their infants except in so far as they are subjective objects". For "by the time mothers become objectively perceived, their infants have become masters of various techniques for indirect communication, the most obvious of which is the use of language" (Winnicott, 1963b, p. 191).

In any case it is not up to the analyst to be "brilliant", like those "too perfect" mothers who understand too well and too quickly what their infant needs and leave no space for his own creativity. It is, if anything, the analyst "recreating" the area which the patient needs, the area necessary for him, which is the area of primary non-integration. This place of the other must be maintained to permit this experience to carry on until "personalisation", instead of breaking up.

In such cases, the work incumbent upon the analyst reminds us of the way that Winnicott considers the process of development as depending on the effective presence of the other. As already quoted, he writes: "The sense of self comes on the basis of an unintegrated state which, however, by definition is not observed and remembered by the individual, and which is lost unless observed and mirrored back by someone who is trusted and who justifies the trust and meets the dependence" (Winnicott, 1971a). Which means that this formless, unintegrated experience will only become a source of personal development if someone is there to reflect it—like the infant who sees himself first in his mother's face, then in a mirror, and retains from this confrontation the feeling of being. We find here the essential task of the analyst: to give back what the patient brings, and to establish a linkage between the scattered elements.

The capacity to be alone

To feel alone, "be alone", is therefore an event which occurs naturally in the life of a child. This established fact leads us on to another of Winnicott's important themes, directly linked to that of "communicating and non-communicating", and that is "the capacity to be alone" (Winnicott, 1958b, p. 29), the title of one of his famous papers published in 1958.

In fact it is about being "alone in the presence of someone", as Winnicott specifies. He asserts from the beginning that this capacity is one of the most important signs of the maturity of emotional development. He writes: "It will be appreciated that actually to be alone is not what I am discussing. A person may be in solitary confinement, and yet not be able to be alone. How greatly he must suffer is beyond imagination. Even so, many people do become able to enjoy solitude before they are out of childhood, and they may even value solitude as a most precious possession" (ibid., p. 30). However this possibility is not obvious. The capacity to be alone, in the sense of real solitude, finds its root in the experience in infancy of a relationship to another who not only stayed at the right distance, but could offer at the right moment the ego support that could contain the experiences that otherwise might have been disintegrating.

"At the right distance" signifies the minimum impingement, which allows the infant to "be", and not to react. And "ego support" describes the effort of metabolisation that gives meaning to the instinctual sensation that the infant goes through. To help us situate this better, Winnicott then invents two terms, which are often difficult to understand: *ego-relatedness* and *id-relationship*. But he wanted to make a distinction between a method of "connection", "liaison" or "re-liaison" to the ego, and a form of "relation" to the id.

We have already seen how the term ego has been a problem for Winnicott with regard to his notion of the psychic apparatus. It seems therefore that when he uses the term ego-relatedness, it relates to a "connection" to the ego. But which ego? It is not clear. At this stage of the infant's development, it could be the ego of the person looking after his needs, the ego of the mother-environment. In his work afterwards, we no longer find the term ego-relatedness, which is a pity, because at the moment of writing this paper, he noted how this "connection to the ego" (of the mother) takes place before any object-relating. In fact the distinction repeats that which exists between mother-environment and mother-object, the first mother being the one we are merged with and the second the one who is the object of drive attacks. This distinction can also be compared with the difference made between the two verbs in English "to like" and "to love". For him, "to like" is in the domain of relating to the ego, and "to love" the domain of the relation to the id.

This support provided by the ego of the mother forms the canvas on which are drawn the instinctual experiences. It is in this framework alone that the instinctual experiences strengthen the structuration of the infant. "It is only when alone (that is to say in the presence of someone) that the infant can discover his own personal life. The infant is able to become unintegrated, to flounder, to be in a state where there is no orientation, to be able to exist for a time being neither a reactor to an external impingement nor an active person with a direction of interest or movement" (Winnicott, 1958b, p. 30). The stage is set for an id-experience: "In the course of time there arrives a sensation or an impulse. In this setting the sensation or impulse will feel real and be truly a personal experience" (p. 31). And from our point of view, it is the neutral reliability of the environment that ensures the conditions for these enriching processes to exist and take place. It relates to a state of solitude and quiet non-integration, with no danger of annihilation, since there is "someone" there who is containing the situation. "A large number of such experiences form the basis for a life that has reality in it instead of futility", writes Winnicott. "The individual who has developed the capacity to be alone is constantly able to rediscover the personal impulse, and the personal impulse is not wasted because the state of being alone is something which (though paradoxically) always implies that someone else is there" (p. 34).

So the capacity to be alone, which is as we have seen, far from being automatically acquired, implies that the individual must first be able to develop an inside world, to rediscover a state of psychic non-integration (that is to say, a state where he can allow himself to be, a state of rest in relation to the transitional area). The framework of the cure must be the place where the patient can experiment and find this capacity to be alone, the indispensable grounds for a capacity to relate.

Silent communication

This is how we arrive at the idea that relations and communications having a real meaning are silent. For Winnicott, it is indispensable that in everyday life there should be moments of silent or secret communication with objects which may be subjective, but which have a feeling of "real", in his sense of the term.

In the same paper, and for reasons which seem today to be obvious, Winnicott dwells on the psychology of those we call mystics. Although we are always inclined to explain away the mystic's retreat to an inner world of introjects, Winnicott wonders if we should not rather understand this "active non-communication" as a way of communicating secretly with personal subjective phenomena to rediscover the core self. This is perhaps what the religious men and women in silent orders are trying to describe. And it is perhaps also what is realised by people who practice meditation. They meditate for many long hours to try to empty their mind of all thought, and they describe the feeling that they have come into contact with a secret core, which is inaccessible to them the rest of the time. They leave these experiences (which are difficult and often painful) with a feeling of self-adequacy. In other words, "At the centre of each person is an incommunicado element, and this is sacred and most worthy of preservation" (Winnicott, 1963b, p. 179).

Every analyst must respect these areas and these specific moments. He must estimate whether such times and such forms of non-communication are due to resistance, in the general sense of the term, or to necessary periods, which are even vital to allow the possibility for eventual access to another way of functioning.

Winnicott drops a bombshell at the end of his article: "Rape, and being eaten by cannibals, these are mere bagatelles as compared with the violation of the self's core." He explains "the hatred people have of psycho-analysis" in general, and in particular the mistrust of adolescents who are so afraid of what they are dreading, the violation of their intimacy. In practice, the analyst must avoid confirming the adolescent's fears. He must expect to be tested. He must be prepared to use communication of an indirect kind and to recognise simple non-communication.

Winnicott had enormous clinical experience with adolescents, and particularly young people who had been "deprived" children. According to him, the adolescent is looking for a personal way to behave in a relationship without compliance (or what he feels it is). The analyst must be careful to give him the space where he can isolate himself without being completely cut off from the world. As Octave Mannoni remarks, "we do not look after an adolescent crisis, we accompany it" (Mannoni, 1984).

CHAPTER NINE

Splitting and dissociated elements

Winnicott's conception of a self composed of several parts leads him to discussions that are among the most difficult of his theories. This is the case for what he calls "masculine elements" and "feminine elements", which he develops in his paper entitled "Creativity and its origins" (1971d), published in 1971. From the beginning, he warns his readers that he uses these terms "masculine and feminine elements", because there is nothing more satisfactory available to him at the moment. Freud had proposed to replace "masculine" and "feminine" by "active" and "passive", but Winnicott considers that "certainly 'active' and 'passive' are not correct terms, and I must continue the argument using the terms that are available" (Winnicott, 1971d, p. 65).

We have already seen how we had similar difficulties while reading the work of Winnicott. In this work we find that a real inventiveness of conceptualisation coexists with what we have to call a certain laxity, a certain approximation in his use of agreed analytical terms. We often feel a sort of annoyance. On the other hand, this approximation of his theories frequently does disservice to his ideas. At the same time, this is just what his writing allows, digression and disagreement, and it is in this sense that Winnicott opens the way to our own creative capacity, in contrast to the many other theories which prevent us from using our own thought process.

Winnicott has a very personal way of allowing us to think as we continue reading his texts. They are never presented as a "whole", compact theory, but as "fragments", "moments" of dream, poetry, that lead us to our field of clinical associations. In other words, he does not slip into dogma. In his writing there is never a statement of truth that has to be accepted as such, but rather a sketch which we have to complete our own way (exactly like the squiggle technique), an outline that opens every possibility.

So what he presents in the paper in question is, as he notes, a "speculation", a speculation which emerged during a moment of the cure. It is a further illustration of his method of working. Winnicott never relates a clinical anecdote as an illustration of his theory. It is rather the opposite that occurs: the clinical anecdote is the start of a process that takes him much further than he anticipated. Throughout his work Winnicott never begins to explain a point of theory that might oblige him to illustrate it by a fragment of the cure. In an opening to what happens in the *"hic et nunc"* of the analytical hour and the interrelation between transference/counter-transference, he is surprised by and questions the material which emerges. In his work on "reverie" (in W. R. Bion's sense) he metabolises what "came into his mind", as Freud said, and so can make headway on the questions raised as he listens to his patients. This way of working, this elaboration which is unexpected, continuous and progressive is a true illustration of the way in which the "thinking apparatus" of the analyst is capable of rendering the β-elements transformed and thinkable, the "thing in itself" brought by the patient (see the theory of W. R. Bion).

I am listening to a girl

This whole new adventure begins during a session with a fully mature patient who had already had many years in analysis with different psychoanalysts. This man is quite satisfied with the changes in his personality up till then. And yet there is something that prevents him from feeling that his analysis is complete. It seems that what he came to analysis for has not yet been attained. And he cannot give up, in spite of his "working at his own analysis for a quarter of a century" (Winnicott, 1971d, p. 65). On the particular day in question—the decisive session—Winnicott hears his patient talk of something which evokes for him the "penis envy" envisaged by Freud at the end of his paper "Analysis terminable and interminable" (1937c) concerning a little girl, and suddenly it occurs to Winnicott that he is listening to a girl, where there is a boy on his couch.

Confused and perplexed, he decides to share this counter-transferential element with his patient, and afterwards to surrender himself to whatever this might mean and his own associations, to try to formulate what has just happened. Here is Winnicott's report:

> On a Friday the patient came and reported much as usual. The thing that struck me on this Friday was that the patient was talking about *penis envy*. I use this term advisedly, and I must invite accept-ance of the fact that this term was appropriate here in view of the material, and of its presentation. Obviously this term, penis envy, is not usually applied in the description of a man.
>
> The change that belongs to this particular phase is shown in the way I handled this. On this particular occasion I said to him: "I am listening to a girl. I know perfectly well that you are a man but I am listening to a girl, and I am talking to a girl, I am telling this girl 'You are talking about penis envy'".
>
> I wish to emphasise that this has nothing to do with homosexuality.
>
> [...]
>
> It was clear to me, by the profound effect of this interpretation, that my remark was in some way apposite, and indeed I would not be reporting this incident in this context were it not for the fact that the work that started on this Friday did in fact break the vicious circle. I had grown accustomed to a routine of good work, good interpre-tation, good immediate results, and then destruction and disillu-sionment that followed each time because of the patient's gradual recognition that something fundamental had remained unchanged; there was this unknown factor which had kept this man working at his own analysis for a quarter of a century. Would his work with me suffer the same fate as his work with the other therapists?
>
> On this occasion there was an immediate effect in the form of intellectual acceptance, and relief, and then there were more remote effects. After a pause, the patient said: 'If I were to tell someone about this girl I would be called mad'.

The matter could have been left there, but I am glad, in view of subsequent events, that I went further. It was my next remark that surprised me, and it clinched the matter. I said: 'It was not that *you* told this to anyone; it is *I* who see the girl and hear a girl talking, when actually there is a man on my couch. The mad person is *myself*'.

I did not have to elaborate this point because it went home. The patient said that he now felt sane in a mad environment. In other words, he was now released from a dilemma. As he said, subsequently, 'I myself could never say (knowing myself to be a man) "I am a girl". *I am not mad that way* [Author's italics]. But you said it, and you have spoken to both parts of me.'

This madness which was mine [Author's italics] enabled him to see himself as a girl *from my position*. He knows himself to be a man, and never doubts that he is a man.

Is it obvious what was happening here? For my part, I have needed to live through a deep personal experience in order to arrive at the understanding I feel I have now reached.

This man and I have been driven to the conclusion (though unable to prove it) that his mother (who is not alive now) saw a girl baby when she saw him as a baby before she came round to thinking of him as a boy. In other words this man had to fit into her idea that her baby would be and was a girl. (He was the second child, the first being a boy.) We have very good evidence from inside the analysis that in her early management of him the mother held him and dealt with him in all sorts of physical ways as if she failed to see him as a male. On the basis of this pattern he later arranged his defences, but it was the mother's "madness" that saw a girl where there was a boy, and this was brought right *into the present* by me having said "It is I who am mad". When he came the next time, he arrived complaining that he was ill, he had had the flu, although he *should have* felt better in himself.

My interpretation continued along the line started up on the Friday before. I said: "You feel as if you ought to be pleased that here was an interesting interpretation of mine that had masculine behaviour. *The girl I am talking to, however, does not want the man released*, and indeed she is not interested in him. What she wants is full acknowledgement of herself and of her own rights over your body. [...] The only end to this analysis that this girl can look for is the discovery that in fact you are a girl." Out of this we can begin to understand his conviction that the analysis could never end.

In the subsequent weeks there was a great deal of material confirming the validity of my interpretation and my attitude, and the patient felt that he could see now that his analysis had ceased to be under doom of interminability.

Later I was able to see that the patient's resistance had now shifted to a denial of the importance of my having said 'It is I who am mad'. He tried to pass this off as just my way of putting things—a figure of speech that could be forgotten. [...] The crux of the problem of management is just here in this interpretation, which I confess I nearly did not allow myself to make. (1971d, p. 66)

The terms of change

We ask ourselves what exactly took place? There was nothing there that we could really call new in the theoretical material proposed, for it concerned material that had already been developed a long time—the concept of psychic bisexuality introduced by Freud, who declared it was common to all human beings. No. Winnicott recognises that "In fact I and my patient had been over this ground before" (Winnicott, 1971d, p. 65). And before that, he adds, "I had never been able to make a really mutative interpretation" (we are reminded that it is James Strachey, Winnicott's analyst, who introduced this term into analytic theory). The material had been worked on time after time, but always in the classical terms of the current theory, in terms of "object relating". He explains (and this is the true innovation): "The first thing I noticed was that I had never before fully accepted the complete dissociation between the man (or woman) and the aspect of the personality that has the opposite sex" (Winnicott, 1971d, p. 69). He had considered this hypothesis until then as simple intellectual knowledge stemming from his training, no more. The importance of this data had never had meaning for him. This is perhaps why he writes: "I found myself with a new edge to an old weapon" (p. 75).

We must make it clear that what Winnicott puts forward has nothing to do with what we call today the difference in "gender". What he promises in this paper refers to identity and existence rather than to sexualism. It is at primary identification level.

Dissociation

In the preceding chapters, we have studied Winnicott's conception of the construction of the psychic apparatus. It is not difficult to see that a dissociation like the one we have just seen is entirely possible in a very early period, when integration is incomplete or partial, so that such an operation becomes a major point of this conception and proceeds in a totally logical manner. Moreover, we recall that these ideas of dissociation and splitting were already present in early Freud, in his work on hysteria. As he already wrote in 1895: "The splitting of consciousness which is so striking is present to a rudimentary degree in every hysteria and a tendency to such a dissociation is the basic phenomenon of this neurosis" (Freud, 1895d). But Freud afterwards made no more mention of this until the end of his work. He takes it up again only after the death of Ferenczi. In between, he will have amply developed various elaborations on the different instances—unconscious, preconscious, and conscious, then id, ego, and superego—and will have privileged repression as a defence mechanism against an unbearable representation for the ego.

And it is only in 1937, in "Analysis terminable and interminable" (1937c) and in 1940, in "Splitting of the ego in the process of defence" (1940e) that Freud starts work again on the idea of splitting. He accepts to consider the split-off as a splitting of the ego and not as a splitting between two instances—between ego and id, for example, or between id and superego, etc. So the split-off appears clearly in the ego as a defence mechanism, different from repression (Lévy, 2006). Before this, it was Ferenczi who made splitting an essential process. His extremely specific clinical practice led him to consider that such a possibility was first caused by trauma, by a commotion which he stated split the personality between a painful, powerless part and a powerful intellectual part which does not want to know. As his work progressed, Ferenczi became more and more precise about this mechanism and went as far as to consider that all splitting can occur at a very early stage (*Ur trauma*). He talks of a tearing apart, a tear in the ego that never heals and grows in time.

We already find here the conceptualisation which interested Winnicott until his clarification of the split-off intellect. And when he raises the question of "babies with high IQ", does he not echo the "wise baby" of Ferenczi? It is this idea that Winnicott took over, and which was so useful in his realisation of the effects caused by the impingements and the establishment of the defence mechanism of the modified self, as a result of what we must call a split-off self.

So we are dealing with two modes of thought: the Freudian mode, which favours repression, and the Ferenczian–Kleinian mode, which favours the splitting. Dissociation[1] does not function like repression. In the process of repression, there is a conflict between the instances of the ego, and we can recognise that it is repression by the defence mechanisms set up to maintain the repression. In contrast, what is characteristic of dissociation, and which at the same time makes it so difficult to perceive, is that there is no conflict. The subject *is* all the elements of his dissociated state. He is totally engaged in each of its aspects, and as a result he cannot establish a relation between his two (or more) dissociated parts. To live each of these states at different moments is not necessarily a problem for the subject. We can even suggest that the conflicting states—of repression—are recognised by the *acting out*, whereas the dissociated states—of splitting—are represented, take place, in the subject's life.

Actualisation of the "madness" of the environment

After the intervention: "I am listening to a girl", Winnicott writes that the patient "felt a sense of relationship with me, and this was extremely vivid. It had to do with identity. The pure female split-off element found a primary unity with me as analyst, and this gave the man a feeling of having started to live" (Winnicott, 1971d). (Masud R. Khan, 1974, also describes one of his female patients, who was not a boy in her "fantasy" but "was" a boy. Part of her was a boy, and she lived it in certain aspects of her life.) And although this patient had always felt like a man in his everyday life, it appeared in therapy that his mother first saw him and treated him like a girl. It was the mother's madness, and it was this that was reactualised in the transfer. He had been a girl in the period of non-differentiation with the environment, the mother environment. What his mother had reflected in her early management of him was the image of the girl she had in her head. He had kept in himself an image of a split-off girl self—a split-off which prevented him from going mad. It was of course the environment which was "mad". But to introduce into analysis the burden of a "mad" environment is very difficult. And yet Winnicott does not hesitate to put forward the idea that this was an indispensable stage.

In a letter of the 17th March 1966 to Herbert Rosenfeld, Winnicott asks what should be done in the event that "when the patient's mother is mad, the patient brings this madness to the transfer." "Is it not true", he adds, "that at some moment or other the patient must find that the analyst is mad?" (Winnicott, 1987a). "Environmental influence, bad or even good, comes into our work as a traumatic idea, intolerable because not operating within the area of the patient's omnipotence" (Winnicott, 1971d, p. 65). This is why the patient said: "I myself could never say (knowing myself to be a man) 'I am a girl.' I am not mad that way. But you said it, and you have spoken to both parts of me" (p. 67). "This madness which was mine enabled him to see himself as a girl *from my position*" (p. 79). Such an intervention shows us what is involved in this kind of work. On the clinical side, the dissociation was almost total for this patient. In cases like these, it is the analyst who has to absorb something of what he has just perceived, to be able to restore it to the patient. For this split-off part must not be simply recognised, it must also be mentioned, be given a presence, and situated *where it is coming from*, that is to say the Other. This is why Winnicott speaks in these terms: "The girl that I was talking to, however, does not want the man released, and indeed she is not interested in him. What she wants is full acknowledgement of herself and of her own rights over your body" (p. 82).

By this example we can see that it is not enough for the analyst simply to listen. On the one hand to listen is not necessarily to contain, and on the other it is about giving back to the patient what he has contributed, in such a way that he can integrate the material once it has been interpreted according to the analytical criteria—"like a mirror that is there to reflect what must be seen", remarks Winnicott. In the example we have studied, he lets his thoughts wander and develop "a speculation", in his terms, on what he calls the "male and female elements in men and women".

Male and female elements in men and women

We must reiterate that Winnicott has warned us that these terms are hardly satisfactory in his eyes, and that he retains them for want of anything better. But we as readers must regret that he did not show more inventiveness in what he was developing. Since misinterpretation is not only easy but almost inevitable. Of course it is not femininity, nor masculinity, nor sexual identity whether feminine or masculine, but "feminine elements" and "masculine elements" that we can find in every human being, whatever their sex (In her remarkable book, Jan Abram, 1996, remarks that these ideas are close to those of Jung on the feminine and masculine aspects of the personality (*anima* and *animus*)). Winnicott writes: "I wish to say that the element that I am calling 'male' [in his text, Winnicott constantly uses the inverted commas to show he is bothered by these terms] does traffic in terms of active relating or passive being related to, each being backed by instinct" (we must remember the meaning that ethology gives to the term instinct). By contrast, "the pure female element relates to the breast (or to the mother) in the sense of *the baby becoming the breast (or mother) in the sense that the object is the subject*. I can see no instinct drive in this" (Winnicott, 1971d, p. 65). This phrase is very enigmatic if we do not take the trouble to dwell upon it further. In reality, it takes us back to what we have already observed, namely that the constitution of the object occurs only from the time it can be external. Before that, Winnicott notes mysteriously "drive has not yet taken up its central position" (Winnicott, 1988).

The drive in fact needs to be able to fix on an object. And at the beginning, the object does not yet exist as an "objective" object. So that the masculine element can act, there must already have been a separation, a distinction between the me and the "not-me". In Winnicott's terms, "As soon as there is the ego organisation available, the baby allows the object the quality of being not-me or separate" (Winnicott, 1971d, p. 65). This baby can then feel the anger resulting from frustration and this anger will reinforce the objectification of the object: "Henceforth, on the male element side, identification needs to be based on complex mental mechanisms, mechanisms that must be given time to appear, to develop, and to become established as part of the new baby's equipment" (p. 80).

One thing is sure

For Winnicott, the female element is primary. It is, he states, in the order of being. It is to be found in an "extremely archaic" time—I would say "primordial"—before the birth and shortly afterwards. For "no sense of self emerges except on the basis of this relating in the sense of Being. This sense of being is something that antedates the idea of being-at-one-with. [... .] Two separate persons can *feel* at one, but here at the place I am examining the baby and the object *are* one" (Winnicott, 1971d, p. 68). And Winnicott adds something very essential: "The term primary identification has perhaps been used for just this that I am describing and I am trying to show how vitally important this first experience is for the initiation of all subsequent experiences of identification" (p. 71).

It is easy to understand such logic after the study of the self he undertook in the preceding chapters. We can even formulate the idea that the "pure female element" is at the heart of what Winnicott calls the true self, and this is the case for all subjects—boys as well as girls—because we are all "born of a woman" (here we are reminded of the famous prediction that weighs on Macbeth, that "none of woman born" will be his murderer. Shakespeare, 1606). "Here one finds a true continuity of generations, being which is passed on from one generation to another, via the female element of men and women and of male and female infants" (this is also what causes Winnicott to say "women always were and always will be").

> Either the mother has a breast that *is*, so that the baby can also *be* when the baby and mother are not yet separated out in the infant's rudimentary mind; or else the mother is incapable of making this contribution, in which case the baby has to develop without the capacity to be, or with a crippled capacity to be (clinically one needs to deal with the case of the baby who has to make do with an identity to a breast that is active, which is a male element breast, but which is not satisfactory for the initial identity which needs a breast that *is*, not a breast that *does*. Instead of "being like", this baby has to "do like" or to be done to, which from our point of view here is the same thing). (Winnicott, 1971d, p. 65, parentheses in original)

"To be ... or not to be"

So this study of the female element defined as "uncontaminated", as "distilled", leads us to this surprising notion in psychoanalysis, that of "being". For Winnicott, the basic female element serves as a departure point regarding the self-discovery and the feeling of existing. In the psycho-analytical field, Winnicott is the only theorist who puts the accent on a "pure female element", the remnants of a primary fusion with the mother, the base of identity and psychic security, which should neither breed fear, nor hatred of women, nor of the mother nor feminism. This is due to the fact that each individual keeps within him the unconscious memory of this moment of his development. We all then have to take on the task of assembling the male and female elements of our own personality. In any case, the ability to live creatively is built up by the balance between the female and male elements in men and women, which mobilises the different posterior identifications to both the father and mother in their various aspects.

To illustrate this, Winnicott embarks upon a very particular study of another Shakespearian character: Hamlet. According to him, in the famous soliloquy which begins "To be or not to be", Hamlet is trying to express the conflict which is in him, following the death of his father, between the female element and the male element that have coexisted harmoniously up until then. From this angle, his cruelty towards Ophelia could be seen as the ruthless rejection of the female element projected onto her. In fact Hamlet cannot resolve his dilemma, which is why he cannot "be or not be". Winnicott ends by saying "After being—doing and being done to. But first, being."

We could moreover, put forward the idea that every human being in the twilight of his life must face old age and death, the female element, like a regression, to find the place he has not reached during his life, but which he is fast approaching.

A new aspect of dissociation

But what Winnicott calls dissociation finds a particular expression in a new idea he introduces in his paper "Dreaming, fantasying and living" (1971c). Winnicott employs the term "fantasying", using as he often does the progressive present.

Fantasying designates an almost compulsive mental activity which we should place almost at the opposite of imagination (1971c, p. 35), like *"rêvasserie"* or something along the lines of "day dream", but none of these is very satisfactory. Day dreaming encompasses a wealth of possible imaginary activity. Whereas for Winnicott, *fantasying* is a sterile activity, a kind of compulsive *rêvasserie*, "what happens, happens immediately, except that it does not happen at all" (p. 42).

Fantasying

Fantasying has nothing to do with the intensity and life of "fanciful", or the creativity of "fantasy". Fantasying is to fantasy what photography is to life. It is an image in black and white, drained of all fantasy. It is an activity closed off, a logjam, where everything becomes blurred as if in a grey, foggy drizzle. To illustrate this new meaning, Winnicott expands upon the case of a woman patient who had since her early infancy been living in such a parallel world, which was neither that of reality nor that of dreaming. She leads a dissociated life, a kind of existence we could call virtual, a world neither imaginary nor dreaming. "At the same time", he writes, "this very thing can be something that belongs to a dissociated state, and it may not become conscious in the sense that there is never a whole person there to be aware of the two or more dissociated states that are present at any one time" (Winnicott, 1971c, p. 41). This is how the woman had lived. "The main part of her existence was taking place when she was doing nothing whatever" (p. 43). This "doing nothing" was masked by certain activities, like playing games which were boring and obsessive. She spent hours shut up at home, playing game after game of patience, with the radio on all the time, with talk and not music as background noise, which she didn't really listen to. And so she lived in this parallel world and carried on in her head "a continuity of fantasying in which omnipotence was retained and wonderful things could be achieved in a dissociated state" (Winnicott, 1971c, p. 35).

For her fantasying was a way she had discovered to escape, get away from herself, never to face an inner reality which could be dangerous or persecutory. However, this woman had rather exceptional talents. "She knows enough about life and living and about her potential to realise that in life terms she is missing the boat, and that she has always been missing the boat" (Winnicott associates here the act of fantasying to manic defence. And further, in 1935, he mentions a woman patient who dreams that she is arriving in a station, "but the train never leaves").

Based on this compulsive activity, we could say that she has written off the creation of a transitional space. We can state without doubt that the act of fantasying is equally a means of finding, or recovering a state of infantile omnipotence. When Winnicott talks of this omnipotence, a moment which must be experienced and then abandoned, he uses the example of a well known game for English children: "I'm the King of the Castle". We must not forget that this is what he hopes for every child at the start of his life: "to create his world, be the god of his world". In his global conception of the development of the infant, it is an essential moment of his structurisation, as essential as the time that follows, when the infant has renounced this omnipotence. This period of disillusion coincides more or less with the beginning of the phase of concern.

The fact remains that for a long time, playing allowed the infant (and the adult he will later become) to relive, for a few moments, similar periods of omnipotence. This is probably why there are people who are "bad losers" even when, in the game they are participating in, there seem to be no high stakes. For these "bad losers", the game, as playful entertainment, doubtless brings about a temporary phase of regression to the period of omnipotence, where they still have to make an effort to control the situation.

The virtual world

We could hypothesise that the compulsive use of video games, or the addiction to television series, is connected with what Winnicott is hinting at by the term fantasying. With the availability today of television series on dvd, some adolescents are capable of spending all their time, days and nights, planted in front of their screens. As one of them said "I'm completely hooked!"

It must be said that these series are very well made, incredibly well done, and designed to encourage addiction. Each episode ends in such a way that it is very difficult not to carry on to watching the next episode. For many adolescents, and also even for adults, there is a real danger of it becoming hypnotic. This parallel world ends up, in effect, by being the real world of psychic activity. But it is a virtual world, which is not an area of the imaginary, since what is presented is a prefabricated world, whether it be the video games or the TV series. And this world can be a trap, just as the act of fantasying is. Incidentally, there are today specialist consultations dedicated to the subject where the addiction to video games is now considered an addiction like any other. According to today's figures for the regular players of video game networks, fifteen per cent of them have a genuine problem, and four per cent suffer from real dependence (Thomas Gahon: communicated during my seminar "Introduction to the work of Winnicott" at the Société de psychanalyse freudienne).

Obviously these players are escaping from reality, the family, the outside world, and they take refuge in the contacts they make in the virtual world of network games. "The games are too well made", said Benjamin, 21, "they give you power, adventure, friendship, love, recognition, and the capacity to influence what is happening. If you don't have any of this in your life, your priorities are topsy turvey" (*Le Monde*, 2003). And Jordan adds: "Outside, it's a tough world, you don't feel like going out. I live on my sofa, with my keyboard on my lap, my bottle of coke and my fags beside me" (*Le Monde*, 2003).

In fact what interests us, as psychoanalysts, about these network games, is that the player creates "an avatar"—this is the term!—who represents himself, and who embarks on the adventure alone, poor, and without weapons. The initiation is harsh. As the struggles, battles, and alliances proceed, he acquires weapons, gold, and power. But instead of being tributary of only one Other from the beginning of the journey, our "hero" gradually creates links with a multitude of other little beings, which of course makes him less vulnerable and less dependent. At first a loner, he is soon included in a group where they use a kind of language. *And it is the language which makes the group!* But to keep up his contacts, he has to be as active as his companions, which means he has to spend as much time as they do in the game. In fact, it is not about showing what an able tactician he is, but to spend as much time as possible in the game, that is "in a relationship". The metaphor speaks for itself! In certain cases, that world becomes the only place where the player feels alive. Everything has been reversed. The virtual has become real life, exactly like Winnicott's woman patient who, he assures us, "fantasying takes over, like an evil spirit"—a good description of what the friends and relatives feel about those who become "addicted" to virtual reality ... . And what they say themselves when they take the step to treatment for addiction. I first realised the possible association between the fantasying that Winnicott explains in his text and the compulsive use of certain video games, when listening to a patient, D, complaining one morning about what she had experienced the evening before when playing "The Sims" (the first simulation of human life, in the terms of their creators).

The world of "The Sims"

The Sims are little virtual characters that we bring to life in a computer, a life that we try to be as near as possible to reality. First we first create them, then we put them as far as possible in a comfortable, functional, and appropriate living space. But D had obviously felt very upset and helpless by her inability to make them act as she wished. She arrived that morning extremely depressed. We must specify here that that the Sims game is designed in such a way that the little characters have a certain self-reliance. In particular, we cannot speed up the time they need to eat, take a shower, go to the toilet, etc. There is what the players call "Sim time", a length of time decided and governed by the machine. And D complained that she could not control these bizarre little characters, just as she also objected that she had to adhere to their timetable, the famous Sim time. This thirty-year-old woman was unmarried, and had been looked after by her grandmother when she was very young, following a long, chaotic infancy with her very young, and disorganised mother. She had experienced a disconnected start in life, a rhythm which was completely out of touch with her needs, a rhythm which all she could do as a newborn baby was to submit to (but at what price?). In time she had managed to build herself up again, but with difficulty. The profession she had chosen—in order to take care of herself?—was that of caring for children, the children of others. But in the evenings, as soon as she got back to her tiny, closed off universe where she was no longer motivated by the lives of other people's children, she seized her computer, and played until she went to bed. She tried desperately to control the Sim time, which continued to be out of her reach, a time that resisted all her attempts to be in charge.

This compulsive playing of the game, together with a compulsive eating habit, lasted for months. In fact, she had never actually spoken of this in sessions, until one day, when she had once again remained powerless in her attempt to control things, she relived the primitive agony of the newborn—which is my hypothesis—and she went to pieces. This day turned out later to be an important moment in the course of her cure. This is one of the reasons Winnicott evokes in his texts for the necessity to go through formlessness, to return to the time before we were "cut out", shaped, put together, "like a dress made from a pattern".

Dreaming and living

Winnicott thus highlights the essential difference that exists between the fantasying on the one hand, and "dreaming" and "living" on the other. He writes: "Dream fits into object-relating in the real world, and living in the real world fits into the dream-world in ways that are quite familiar, especially to psychoanalysts" (Winnicott, 1971c, p. 35). On the other hand, fantasying remains an isolated phenomenon, which absorbs energy but which participates neither in dream nor in life. And, he concludes, "dreaming and living have been seen to be of the same order." In other words, the dream is closer to life than fantasying. To anticipate by imagination, to "dream" something which is going to happen, is according to him, a part of health. It may be "an imaginative exploration of the world and of the place where dream and life are the same thing" (p. 48). To dream is to live!

Note

1. Split-off (definition of Rycroft): a state in which two or more psychic processes coexist without necessarily being linked together or integrated. We find this field of thought in Edward Glover, Erik Erickson, Helene Deutsch, Ronald Laing, Harold Searles, etc.

CONCLUSION

I could have called this book "Introduction to the meta-psychology of Donald W. Winnicott", but this title, which is a bit pompous, is hardly suitable to describe an oeuvre which is simply composed of questions and paradoxes. "My contribution is to ask for a paradox to be accepted and tolerated and respected, and for it not to be resolved. By flight to split-off intellectual functioning it is possible to resolve the paradox, but the price of this is the loss of the value of the paradox itself" (Winnicott, 1971a, p. 11). Replying to questions freezes them, to try to resolve the paradox reduces the field of creativity. The important thing is that the question can be posed, not the reply to it. The inspiration is in the question itself.

We have followed the course of the baby who comes into the world and who goes from absolute dependence to relative dependence, and then to independence, to create himself as a subject by renouncing the object. We have equally seen how the majority of Winnicott's intuitions have been confirmed by the giant strides made in the understanding of the newborn baby's world. His most important paradox remains no doubt that the world is found by the infant, but that it had to be there, waiting to be found. The encounter with this world is mediatised

131

from the start by the other, and the relation we have with the world and with the other is inscribed in the space of the found–created from the beginning. This is the area of necessary and positive illusion. The hallucination, which only just precedes the encounter with the world, must become part of it. It is because this process has already taken place "until completion" (Winnicott, 1988, p. 166) that I can bear this encounter being deferred without being annihilated. Primary creativity is rooted here, in the potential area which at the same time unites and separates inner and outer reality, and which permits the perpetual movement from one to the other, a movement which is life.

Any failure in this process constitutes what Winnicott calls an impingement, a non-event, a trace of which remains inscribed in the subject. This absence, this "void", this lack (in the sense of something missing) brings a feeling of primary distress that reactivates throughout life on certain occasions. And this non-encounter, this void trauma, this negative trauma, this Ur trauma, leaves its mark on the construction of subjectivity.

It leaves a trace, a weakness, a "fault line" that indicates a split-off self and the setting up of defence mechanisms, inaugurating a specific relationship of the subject to the world. In "Concept of a healthy individual" (1967b), Winnicott tries to give us an idea of the different ways in which this relationship, "specific" to oneself and to the world, can be set up:

> I find it useful to divide the world of people into two classes. There are those who were never "let down" as babies and who are to that extent candidates for the enjoyment of life and of living. There are also those who did suffer traumatic experience of the kind that results from environmental letdown; and who must carry with them all their lives the memories (or the material for memories) of the state they were in at moments of disaster. These are candidates for lives of storm and stress and perhaps illness.
>
> We recognise the existence of those who lost grip of the tendency towards healthy development, and whose defences are organised in rigidity, the rigidity being itself a guarantee against forward movement. We cannot extend our meaning of the word "health" to cover this state of affairs.
>
> There is a middle group, however. In a fuller exposition of the psychomorphology of health, we would include those who carry

round with them experiences of unthinkable or archaic anxiety, and who are defended more or less successfully against remembering such anxiety, but who nevertheless use any opportunity that turns up to become ill and have a breakdown in order to approach that which was unthinkably terrible. The breakdown only seldom leads to a therapeutic result, but the positive element in the breakdown must be acknowledged. Sometimes the breakdown does lead to a kind of cure, and then the word "health" turns up again.

There seems to be a tendency towards healthy development that persists even here, and if these people in my second category can manage to hitch on to this tendency towards development, even if late, they may yet make good. We can then include these among the healthy. Healthy by hook or by crook. (Winnicott, 1967b, p. 22)

Winnicott was convinced that a wide diffusion of his ideas amongst a public of non-psychoanalysts—laymen!—would help a "prevention" of neuroses. He affirms "Prophylaxis against psychosis is therefore the responsibility of the paediatricians, did they but know it" (Winnicott, 1952b, p. 219).

He defined himself as "being a paediatrician with a knack for getting mothers to tell me about their children" (Winnicott, 1962a, p. 172).

To support this idea of prophylaxis, he used to give talks on the BBC, which gave him enormous pleasure. It was the same with his consultations at the Paddington Green Hospital. "I quickly learned to think of my clinic as a department for the management of maternal and paternal hypochondria" (Winnicott, 1958a, p. 50. His biographers estimate that in the course of his career he had met with about 60,000 families, which is a colossal amount!).

His "therapeutic consultations" effectively constituted "his" way of working with families with whom he knew he could not for diverse reasons (financial, social, cultural, geographic) undertake a long therapy. Therefore in two or three consultations—but sometimes in only one—he tried to reach the point where "the processes had frozen." With the aid of the squiggle game technique he entered into communication with the infant which intensified until it arrived at the "crowning moment", the instant when he briefly became a "subjective object", when both he and his patient found themselves in contact with the origin of everything—"the significant moment is that at which the child surprises himself or herself" (Winnicott, 1971g).

In fact Winnicott loved being magic. It was perhaps his blind spot—and not his maternal identification, as is often said. He had to reach the end of his life before he realised it, and thus to develop his thoughts on the necessity for the analyst to allow himself to be used; for use of the therapist by the patient allows the patient to get rid of the idea that he has of the therapist as a magician. It just shows what an incredible clinician he was, to have continued to follow up his ideas until his last breath!

Throughout his life he also maintained that for certain patients, the only solution was to relive what had already been experienced. "There is no end unless the bottom of the trough has been reached, unless *the thing feared has been experienced*" (Winnicott, 1963a, p. 87). But he warns: "A main task of the analyst of any patient is to maintain objectivity in regard to all that the patient brings, and a special case of this is the analyst's need to be able to hate the patient objectively" (Winnicott, 1947, p. 194). For Winnicott considers that the analysts' hatred of the patient, like the hatred of the mother towards her infant, needs to be recognised and developed. Since, he stresses, "should the analyst show love, he will surely at the same moment kill the patient" (p. 197).

This is one of the principal points in his extremely original conception of the cure. All these clinical aspects will be dealt with in a further book.

REFERENCES

Abram, J. (1996). *The Language of Winnicott: A Dictionary of Winnicott's Use of Words*. London: Karnac.

Avrane, P. (2007). *Eloge de la gourtmandise*. Paris: Editions de la Martinière.

Bettelheim, B. (1983). *Freud and Man's Soul*. New York: Knopf.

Bion, W. R. (1962). *Learning from Experience*. London: Maresfield.

Castoriadis-Aulagnier, P. (2001). *The Violence of Interpretation: From Pictogram to Statement*. The New Library of Psychoanalysis. London: Routledge.

Chapsal, M. (1994). *Ce que m'a appris Françoise Dolto*. Paris: Fayard.

Clancier, A. & Kalmanovich, J. (1987). *Winnicott and Paradox: From Birth to Creation*. London: Tavistock.

Damasio, A. R. (1999). *The Feeling of What Happens: Body and Emotion in the Making of Consciousness*. New York: Harcourt.

Ferenczi, S. (1982). *Œuvres Complètes Volume 4*. Paris: Payot.

Freud, S. (1895) [1950a]. Project for a scientific psychology. *S. E., 1*: 295–410. London: Hogarth.

Freud, S. (1895d). *Studies on Hysteria. S. E., 2*. London: Hogarth.

Freud, S. (1908e). Creative writers and day dreaming. *S. E., 9*: 141–154. London: Hogarth.

Freud, S. (1914c). On narcissism, an introduction. *S. E., 14*: 67–102. London: Hogarth.

Freud, S. (1920g). *Beyond the Pleasure Principle. S. E., 18*: 1–64. London: Hogarth.

Freud, S. (1923b). The ego and the id. *S. E., 19*: 19–27. London: Hogarth.

Freud, S. (1926d). *Inhibitions, Symptoms and Anxiety. S. E., 20*: 87–156. London: Hogarth.

Freud, S. (1933a). *New Introductory Lectures in Psycho-Analysis. S. E., 22*: 81–111. London: Hogarth.

Freud, S. (1937c). Analysis terminable and interminable. *S. E., 23*: 209–216. London: Hogarth.

Freud, S. (1940e). Splitting of the ego in the process of defence. *S. E., 23*: 271–275. London: Hogarth.

Green, A. (2001). The dead mother. In: *Life Narcissism, Death Narcissism*. London: Free Association.

Guntrip, H. (1975). My experience of analysis with Fairbairn and Winnicott. In: *International Review of Psycho-Analysis Volume 2*, (pp. 145–156).

Huston, N. (2008). *Fault Lines*. London: Atlantic.

Jung, C. G. (1963). *Memories, Dreams, Reflexions*. New York: Pantheon.

Kahr, B. (1996). *D. W. Winnicott, A Biographical Portrait*. London: Karnac.

Khan, M. M. R. (1974). To hear with eyes: Clinical notes on body as subject and object. In: *The Privacy of the Self* (pp. 234–250). London: Hogarth.

Khan, M. M. R. (1989). Introduction. In: *Holding and Interpretation: Fragment of an Analysis*. London: Karnac.

Lacan, J. (1988). *The Seminar, Book II: The Ego in Freud's Theory and in the Technique of Psychoanalysis* (1954–1955). New York: W. W. Norton & Co.

Le Monde (2003). Les fondues du virtuel, 11th January 2003.

Le Monde (2008). Retrouver son doudou, 21st March 2008.

Lévy, F. (2006). L'après-coup, selon Freud. In: *Lettres de la SPF, n°15* (pp. 113–124). Paris: CampagnePremière.

Little, M. (1985). Winnicott working in areas where psychotic anxieties predominate: A personal record. In: *Free Associations, Volume 1, Issue 3* (pp. 9–42).

Mannoni, O. (1977). Winnicott. In: *L'Arc n°69*.

Mannoni, O. (1980). *Un commencement qui n'en finit pas*. Paris: Seuil.

Mannoni, O. (1984). La crise d'adolescence. In: *La Crise d'adolescence*. Paris: Denoël.

McDougall, J. (1995). *The Many Faces of Eros*. London: Free Association.

O'Dwyer de Macedo, H. (1994). *De l'Amour à la Pensée*. Paris: l'Harmattan.

O'Dwyer de Macedo, H. (2008). *Lettres à un Jeune Psychanalyste*. Paris: Stock.

Phillips, A. (1988). *Winnicott*. London: Fontana.

Rodman, F. R. (2003). *Winnicott: His Life and Work*. Cambridge, MA: Perseus.

Roustang, F. (1994). *Qu'est-ce que l'hypnose?* Paris: Minuit.

Shakespeare, W. (1606). *Macbeth*, Act IV, Scene 1.

Stern, D. (1985). *The Interpersonal World of the Infant: A View from Psychoanalysis and Development*. Basic Books.

Verny, T. (1981). *The Secret Life of the Unborn Child*. New York: Dell.

Winnicott, C. (1965). D. W. W., A reflection. In: C. Winnicott, R. Shepherd & M. Davis (Eds.), *Psycho-Analytic Explorations* (pp. 1–18). London: Karnac, 1989.

Winnicott, D. W. (1931). *Clinical Notes on Disorders of Childhood*. London: Heinemann.

Winnicott, D. W. (1935). The manic defence. In: *Through Paediatrics to Psychoanalysis* (pp. 129–144). London: Karnac, 1984.

Winnicott, D. W. (1941). The observation of infants in a set situation. In: *Through Paediatrics to Psychoanalysis* (pp. 52–69). London: Karnac, 1984.

Winnicott, D. W. (1945a). Primitive emotional development. In: *Through Paediatrics to Psychoanalysis* (pp. 145–156). London: Karnac, 1984.

Winnicott, D. W. (1945b). What about father? In: *The Child and the Family*. London: Tavistock.

Winnicott, D. W. (1947). Hate in the counter-transference. In: *Through Paediatrics to Psychoanalysis* (pp. 194–203). London: Karnac, 1984.

Winnicott, D. W. (1948). Reparation in respect of mother's organised defence against depression. In: *Through Paediatrics to Pyschoanalysis* (pp. 91–96). London: Karnac, 1984.

Winnicott, D. W. (1949a). Birth memories, birth trauma and anxiety. In: *Through Paediatrics to Psychoanalysis* (pp. 174–193). London: Karnac, 1984.

Winnicott, D. W. (1949b). Mind and its relation to the psycho-soma. In: *Through Paediatrics to Psychoanalysis* (pp. 243–254). London: Karnac, 1984.

Winnicott, D. W. (1950). The Deprived child and how he can be compensated for loss of family life. In: C. Winnicott, R. Shepherd & M. Davis (Eds.), *Deprivation and Delinquency* (pp. 172–188). London: Tavistock, 1984.

Winnicott, D. W. (1950s). Ideas and definitions. In: C. Winnicott, R. Shepherd & M. Davis (Eds.), *Psycho-Analytic Explorations* (pp. 43–44). London: Karnac, 1989.

Winnicott, D. W. (1952a). Anxiety associated with insecurity. In: *Through Paediatrics to Psychoanalysis* (pp. 97–100). London: Karnac, 1984.

Winnicott, D. W. (1952b). Psychoses and child care. In: *Through Paediatrics to Psychoanalysis* (pp. 219–228). London: Karnac, 1984.

Winnicott, D. W. (1953). Transitional objects and transitional phenomena. In: *Playing and Reality* (pp. 1–34). London: Routledge, 1971.

Winnicott, D. W. (1954a). Metapsychological and clinical aspects of regression within the psychoanalytical set-up. In: *Through Paediatrics to Psychoanalysis* (pp. 278–295). London: Karnac, 1984.

Winnicott, D. W. (1954b). The depressive position in normal emotional development. In: *Through Paediatrics to Psychoanalysis* (pp. 262–277). London: Karnac, 1984.

Winnicott, D. W. (1954c). Letter to Harry Guntrip, 20th July 1954. In: *The Spontaneous Gesture*, (pp. 75–76). Cambridge, MA: Harvard University Press.

Winnicott, D. W. (1956). Primary maternal preoccupation. In: *Through Paediatrics to Psychoanalysis* (pp. 300–305). London: Karnac, 1984.

Winnicott, D. W. (1957a). Further thoughts on babies as persons. In: *The Child, the Family and the Outside World: Studies in Developing Relationships*. London: Tavistock.

Winnicott, D. W. (1957b). Letter to Augusta Bonnard, 1 Oct. 1957. In: *The Spontaneous Gesture*, (pp. 116–117). Cambridge, MA: Harvard University Press.

Winnicott, D. W. (1958a). Family affected by depressive illness in one or both parents. In: *The Family and Individual Development* (pp. 50–60). London: Tavistock, 1965.

Winnicott, D. W. (1958b). The capacity to be alone. In: *The Maturational Processes and the Facilitating Environment* (pp. 29–36). London: Karnac, 1984.

Winnicott, D. W. (1958c). Child analysis in the latency period. In: *The Maturational Processes and the Facilitating Environment* (pp. 115–123). London: Karnac, 1984.

Winnicott, D. W. (1960a). The theory of the parent–infant relationship. In: *The Maturational Processes and the Facilitating Environment* (pp. 37–55). London: Karnac, 1984.

Winnicott, D. W. (1960b). Ego distortion in terms of true and false self. In: *The Maturational Processes and the Facilitating Environment* (pp. 140–152). London: Karnac, 1984.

Winnicott, D. W. (1962a). A personal view of the Kleinian contribution. In: *The Maturational Processes and the Facilitating Environment* (pp. 171–178). London: Karnac, 1984.

Winnicott, D. W. (1962b). Providing for the child in health and crisis. In: *The Maturational Processes and the Facilitating Environment* (pp. 64–72). London: Karnac, 1984.

Winnicott, D. W. (1962c). Ego integration in child development. In: *The Maturational Processes and the Facilitating Environment* (pp. 56–63). London: Karnac, 1984.

Winnicott, D. W. (1963a). Fear of breakdown. In: C. Winnicott, R. Shepherd & M. Davis (Eds.), *Psycho-Analytic Explorations* (pp. 87–95). London: Karnac, 1989.

Winnicott, D. W. (1963b). Communicating and not communicating leading to a study of certain opposites. In: *The Maturational Processes and the Facilitating Environment* (pp. 179–192). London: Karnac, 1984.

Winnicott, D. W. (1963c). Psychiatric disorder in terms of infantile maturational processes. In: *The Maturational Processes and the Fahome is wherecilitating Environment* (pp. 230–241). London: Karnac, 1984.

Winnicott, D. W. (1964a). Psychosomatic illness in its positive and negative aspects. In: C. Winnicott, R. Shepherd & M. Davis (Eds.), *Psycho-Analytic Explorations* (pp. 103–114). London: Karnac, 1989.

Winnicott, D. W. (1964b). The concept of the false self. In: *Home is Where We Start From*, (pp. 65–70). London: Penguin, 1986.

Winnicott, D. W. (1964c). C. G. Jung, review of memories, dreams, reflexions. In: C. Winnicott, R. Shepherd & M. Davis (Eds.), *Psycho-Analytic Explorations* (pp. 482–493). London: Karnac, 1989.

Winnicott, D. W. (1965). New light on children's thinking. In: C. Winnicott, R. Shepherd & M. Davis (Eds.), *Psycho-Analytic Explorations* (pp. 152–157). London: Karnac, 1989.

Winnicott, D. W. (1966). The ordinary devoted mother. In: *Babies and Their Mothers* (pp. 3–14). London: Free Association, 1988.

Winnicott, D. W. (1967a). Mirror-role of mother and family in child development. In: *Playing and Reality* (pp. 149–159). London: Routledge, 1971.

Winnicott, D. W. (1967b). Concept of a healthy individual. In: C. Winnicott, R. Shepherd & M. Davis (Eds.), *Home is Where We Start From* (pp. 22–38). London: Penguin, 1986.

Winnicott, D. W. (1967c). D. W. W. on D. W. W. In: C. Winnicott, R. Shepherd & M. Davis (Eds.), *Psycho-Analytic Explorations* (pp. 569–582). London: Karnac, 1989.

Winnicott, D. W. (1968a). Communication between infant and mother, and mother and infant, compared and contrasted. In: C. Winnicott, R. Shepherd & M. Davis (Eds.), *Babies and their Mothers* (pp. 89–103). London: Free Association, 1988.

Winnicott, D. W. (1968b). Playing: its theoretical status in the clinical situation. In: *International Journal of Psychoanalysis Vol. 49, n°4* (pp. 591–599).

Winnicott, D. W. (1969). The mother–infant experience of mutuality. In: C. Winnicott, R. Shepherd & M. Davis (Eds.), *Psycho-Analytic Explorations* (pp. 251–260). London: Karnac, 1989.

Winnicott, D. W. (1970a). On the basis for self in body. In: C. Winnicott, R. Shepherd & M. Davis (Eds.), *Psycho-Analytic Explorations* (pp. 261–283). London: Karnac, 1989.

Winnicott, D. W. (1970b). Living creatively. In: *Home is Where We Start From* (pp. 39–54). London: Penguin, 1986.

Winnicott, D. W. (1970c). The cure. In: *Home is Where We Start From* (pp. 112–120). London: Penguin, 1986.

Winnicott, D. W. (1971a). *Playing and Reality*. London: Routledge, 1971.

Winnicott, D. W. (1971b). Playing: creative activity and the search for the self. In: *Playing and Reality* (pp. 71–86). London: Routledge, 1971.

Winnicott, D. W. (1971c). Dreaming, fantasying and living. A case history describing a primary dissociation. In: *Playing and Reality* (pp. 35–50). London: Routledge, 1971.

Winnicott, D. W. (1971d). Creativity and its origins. In: *Playing and Reality* (pp. 65–85). London: Routledge, 1971.

Winnicott, D. W. (1971e). The place where we live. In: *Playing and Reality* (pp. 104–110). London: Routledge, 1971.

Winnicott, D. W. (1971f). The use of an object and relating through identifications. In: *Playing and Reality* (pp. 86–94). London: Routledge, 1971.

Winnicott, D. W. (1971g). *Therapeutic Consultations in Child Psychiatry*. London: Hogarth.

Winnicott, D. W. (1971h). Letter to Mme Jeannine Kalmanovitch, 19th Jan. 1971. In: *Nouvelle Revue de psychanalyse*, 1971, 3.

Winnicott, D. W. (1984). C. Winnicott, R. Shepherd & M. Davis, *Deprivation and Delinquency*. London: Tavistock.

Winnicott, D. W. (1986a). *Holding and Interpretation: Fragment of an Analysis*. London: Hogarth.

Winnicott, D. W. (1986b). C. Winnicott, R. Shepherd & M. Davis (Eds.), *Home is Where We Start From: Essays by a Psychoanalyst*. Harmondsworth: Penguin.

Winnicott, D. W. (1987a). F. R. Rodman (Ed.), *The Spontaneous Gesture*. Cambridge, MA: Harvard University Press.

Winnicott, D. W. (1987b). Preliminary notes for "communication between infant and mother, and mother and infant, compared and contrasted". In: *Babies and their Mothers*, (pp. 107–109). London: Free Association, 1988.

Winnicott, D. W. (1988). C. Bollas, M. Davis & R. Shepherd (Eds.), *Human Nature*. London: Free Association.

Winnicott, D. W. (1989). C. Winnicott, R. Shepherd & M. Davis (Eds.), *Psycho-Analytic Explorations*. London: Karnac, 1989.

INDEX